A Lad from Liverpool

Life Stories

Derek Hughes

CENTRAL PARK SOUTH PUBLISHING

Published by Central Park South Publishing 2023
www.centralparksouthpublishing.com

Copyright © Derek Hughes, 2023

Typesetting and e-book formatting services by Victor Marcos

ISBN:
978-1-956452-29-7 (pbk)
978-1-956452-30-3 (hbk)
978-1-956452-31-0 (ebk)

For Mal

LIFE STORIES BY DEREK HUGHES

PART 3

PART 4

A Word to the Reader

I started writing these stories a number of years ago without any intention of making them into a book.

To me they were sort of a time machine that could transport me back through the years to relive parts of what has been a long and happy life.

This book is neither a memoir nor an autobiography, but simply a collection of stories describing episodes in my life that for some reason resonated with me.

Many people may not appear in these pages. This does not diminish their importance in my life story.

I was lucky enough to have wonderful parents, a close-knit family, two long and loving marriages and enough laughter to last more than one lifetime.

However, before all this wanders into the realm of too good to be true, I am fully aware that no one lives a life unscathed—the reader will also find setbacks, loss, and disappointment in these pages.

So, take these stories for what they are. I do hope you enjoy reading them as much as I did living them.

—Derek Hughes

ACKNOWLEDGMENTS

My thanks to those who helped me bring *A Lad from Liverpool* to publication.

Gay Walley, who was so helpful to me with my first book *Absolute Beginnings,* was again at my side.

My wife Helen, my cheerleader in all things, was always there with her usual enthusiasm and encouragement.

Linda Langton and the staff at *Central Park South Publishing*, especially Lindsay Watson, for their patience and guidance.

I reserve my biggest thank you to my daughter, Jenny, who was tireless in her determination to help me complete this project.

PART 1

A Child's Life in Wartime Liverpool

I grew up in a large, poor, happy family in a working-class area of Liverpool, England during the 1940's. Born in 1934, I was one of seven children—five boys and two girls. I was somewhat in the middle with two older siblings and four younger ones.

We lived at 61A King Street, a small Government subsidized house in the Liverpool dock area. Some of the other houses were even smaller, built in the 19th century. They were actually slums, but nobody called them that until they were torn down after the war. However, on the basis of "in the land of the blind the one-eyed man is king," we were not too badly off. We even had a bath. How was that for luxury?

In my neighborhood, the houses were small, and the families were large. Every family seemed to have at least four children (a kind of entry fee to the neighborhood), so our spilling out into the street to play seemed the obvious thing to do. The alternative was being confined to the cramped spaces of our modest homes. Our house was on a corner, strategically situated as a meeting place for all the neighborhood kids to gather, and there were lots of us. There were few cars around, and the streets teemed with children shouting, dogs barking, and housewives chattering – a street symphony playing every day.

My mother was a small, frail, dark woman, almost gypsy-like in appearance, with a Welsh / Celtic background. She read the tea leaves of friends and family, the predictions from which were fairly vague. Nevertheless, it granted her a certain status.

Mother Agnes, "Aggie" and father William, "Bill"

She had a wonderful sense of humor, but her reaction to anything she found comical was to howl with laughter and, at the same time, flail her arms and push at anyone in the vicinity. Needless to say, those in the know always gave her a wide berth when someone began telling a joke. My sister, Angela, still does the same thing.

My father, on the other hand, was quite different. While my mother was lively, he was quiet and restrained. He was good-humored, though, and enjoyed the lively interactions among his noisy, robust family. He absolutely adored my mother, but he was anything but demonstrative. I never saw him hug or kiss her, but his love shone through so clearly that even we saw it, as young as we were. My mother was quite the opposite. She would sit on his knee in front of the family and smother him with affection, kissing his bald head just to provoke an embarrassed smile onto his face.

As children, there were sins that would be forgiven and certain behavior that might be tolerated. We all knew, however, that the one thing we could not do was to cause my mother stress or anxiety.

That was the unpardonable sin—woe betide anyone who upset her. Being kids, we did of course, but paid the price when my father came home. His zealous protection stemmed from his concern for her health. She had a very weak heart and would be under a doctor's care most of her life, although it never seemed to daunt her spirit or stop her from enjoying herself.

When World War II was declared, life changed dramatically for us as a family, as it did for millions of others. My father went into the army, and this put a great strain on my mother, both financially and physically. She now only had a soldier's pay to support our large family and had to control her boisterous brood without a strong loving husband by her side.

For us kids, though, it was all very exciting. Air raid shelters were built, gas drills organized, and the streets began to fill with soldiers, sailors, and airmen from all over the world. It all seemed like one of the games we played in the street. During the gas drills, we would look like creatures from another planet and would giggle into our already suffocating gas masks.

Then the war began in earnest, and we started to experience the real thing. Hitler, after having his overtures

Schoolchildren learn to put on gas masks, 1939. © Alamy

for alliance with Britain rejected, acted with a fury which we all agreed took petulance to another level. He ordered the mass bombings of Britain's cities and civilian population. Liverpool, as a major seaport, was particularly vulnerable and since the streets around us were only a short distance from the docks, we suffered a great deal from the raids, or the "Blitz" as it was called.

Every night the air raid warnings would begin their whine and my mother would rush up to the bedrooms to scoop the youngest children into her arms while the rest of us would trudge sleepily behind as we made our way to the shelter in our backyard. The Government-built shelter was only half underground, covered with a corrugated steel roof which could withstand pieces of shrapnel but was hardly protection against the bombs.

The shelter was dark and dank, with only candles for light. Some of us found it impossible to sleep, so my mother would talk to us in an effort to take our minds off all the noise and chaos outside. Periodically, an air raid warden would pop into the shelter to check in on us. He would then give my mother the latest news on which houses had been hit, and the inevitable casualties that resulted.

I do not recall being really frightened. I must have been caught up in the excitement of it all. Besides, I felt safe in our own little bunker with my mother, or "me mam," close by. If I had known how fragile our so-called haven really was, I might have felt differently. Even the shriek of the bombs became a game in which we tried to guess where the bombs would drop. I am sure that my mother was terrified inside, but she hid her tension well.

The day after a raid was always exciting. We would leave very early for school in order to look for pieces of shrapnel. The largest and hottest pieces were the grand prizes in that particular war game. Eventually, the raids tapered off and we spent less and less time in the shelter and more and more time in our beds.

At the end of the war, the men came back from the armed forces, and we had our father home again. An air of comparative prosperity took hold, even in the relatively poor area in which we lived. Two of my brothers were old enough to have jobs bringing money into the house. The street activity continued, but it felt much lighter and more carefree. Was it because we'd all had this shared experience and survived it? Who knows? But there was no doubt that life after the war changed for everyone. It certainly had for me.

Let's see what the next chapter brings and please, a little less noise.

Children playing street games, 1945. © Alamy

Anderson Shelter, UK. © Alamy

Civilians and rescue workers search through the wreckage in Liverpool
following a bomb raid during the blitz, 1940. © Alamy

Young residents amidst the ruins of their home celebrate VE Day
marking the end of the war in Europe, May 1945 © Alamy

Ain't Misbehavin'

At around 7:00 p.m. my mother always gave ample warning to the younger kids that it was time for bed, anticipating all the arguments, balking and general push-back against it. My brother, Cyril, age nine, my sister Angela, age seven, and myself, age ten, would hear the shouts and laughter of the kids in the street and, as usual, we wondered why we had to leave all the fun. Some of my friends would be up very late and only went home when they wanted to. This was not so in our house, although our bedtime routine was driven not by discipline but by exhaustion.

My mother was in poor health and was usually extremely tired at the end of the day. My dad was at work and was often home late, so she had to cope alone with her six children, and all the stresses and strains that this entailed.

"All the other kids are playing outside, why can't we?" said a mutinous voice in the corner. My mother would then tell us in a tired but still sharp voice: "If their parents don't care, that's their problem. And you have school tomorrow. Besides, I'm very tired looking after you lot all day and I want some peace and quiet. So no more arguing." Up the stairs we trudged in our nightshirts, carrying a bucket for our needs in the night.

Our house had three small bedrooms. My parents and my baby sister Dorothy were in the front room, my two older brothers, Bill and Stanley, were in a side bedroom, and Angela, Cyril, and I were in the back bedroom. Our room had a large double bed and not much else except a battered chest of drawers in the corner.

The sleeping arrangements were such that my brother and I slept vertically at the head of the bed and my sister slept horizontally at the bottom. On most nights, peace would reign since we were usually tired enough to quickly go to sleep. But there were some nights when the natives were restless.

The situation was rife with conflicts and tension. In the bed at such close quarters, one could be kicked, accidentally or otherwise, then covers would get pulled off, beginning a tug of war which escalated into scuffles between my brother and myself, and my sister crying at the bottom of the bed saying "Mam! Our Derek and Cyril are fighting!"

My mother would then shout her first warning: "Your dad will be home soon and if I tell him what's been going on, you know what will happen!"

Now that gave room for pause. My dad could get very upset, but not for himself. It was the fact that my mother was being bothered. This he would not tolerate. Thus, with the warning ringing in our ears, we tried to settle down. But my brother and I were on a roll, and inevitably the Bedclothes Wars started up again, along with another round of fighting, pulling, and kicking.

And then...

"I'm home and I'm coming up there to make sure you get to sleep."

The cavalry in the form of my father had arrived. He burst into the room as we lay quietly, giving a poor imitation of being fast asleep. "Good," he said, "because if I have to come up here again it will mean the belt."

Ah, the belt. Dad often used the threat of using his belt. But we had never actually seen him do it. Oh yes, he would make grand gestures of grabbing at the buckle and sometimes he would even unfasten it. One time he actually took the belt off, but I never remember him using it for the Dickensian punishment he had threatened. Nevertheless, there was always that possibility, so we figured we had better play it safe. Besides, my father could get really angry, and this was obviously one of those occasions. We heard his footsteps descending the stairs, and when he was about halfway down, he heard...

"AH SHURRUP"!

What on earth possessed me to shout that out? The words seemed to hang in the air, then fly out of the bedroom door and down the stairs to overtake my Dad. My brother gave a gasp of fear, and my sister began to cry. They couldn't believe this incredible act of disobedience. No one spoke to my father like that and lived to tell the tale, or so the story goes.

We could hear my father's footsteps bounding up the stairs, then the door to the bedroom flew open and he burst in. My sister by this time was in hysterics under the bedclothes, my brother, loyal to the end, was shouting repeatedly, "It was our Derek, Dad, it wasn't me!"

I dove under the bedclothes, trying to burrow my way down and become one with the mattress. In fact, we were all now hidden under the bedding. This left a handy target of three bottoms for my father, who by this time had indeed taken off the famous belt and was slapping away at our behinds but only managing to kick up dust from the bed covers. Amid the chaos and what might laughingly be called violence, I'm sure that there must have been a trace of a smile on my Dad's face.

Soon there was silence except for the whimpering under the bedclothes.

"Now get to sleep, and no more messing about!"

Dad went downstairs and I could almost imagine the scene when he went to my mother, who would look at him anxiously and ask, "Ah, ye didn't hurt them did ye, Bill?"

And Dad looking rather smug and saying, "No, but I bloody will next time!"

EVACUEE ADVENTURE

The year was 1941 and I was seven years old. My father was away serving in the British Army.

Our house was only a few streets away from a major dock area, which was a prime target for German bombing raids. These raids were constant— first at night, and then the daylight bombing would begin on England's major cities, including mine. As soon as the air raid warnings started during the day, we would run to the nearest

Derek, 1941 (Age 7)

air raid shelter and stay there until the "All Clear" siren rang out. We never went anywhere without our gas masks.

At the start of the war, the British Government had prepared a plan called "Operation Pied Piper" which called for the evacuation of children in the London area if and when German bombing raids began. As the "Blitz" extended beyond the capital, this evacuation plan was used in more and more cities.

My older brother Bill was thirteen at the time and was the first to go. He ended up with a family in the county of Shropshire. My mother was then advised that my older brother Stan, who was eleven, and I were to be evacuated together. The other children in the family were considered too young to be sent away.

The day came for us to leave. I remember being very miserable at the whole idea of leaving my family and my home no matter how dangerous the British Government thought it was.

My brother and I were sent to a small country village not far from Liverpool called Aughton. It was tranquil and quiet, and despite being only twenty-five miles from my home, it was a million miles away from the war.

We were to stay in a large house owned by a retired colonel. It had a beautiful, manicured lawn and a large conservatory. There were two maids to help take care of us. They wore black and white starched uniforms and tried their best to make us feel at home, but to no avail. The only time we saw the colonel was when he was walking by. He would give us a wave but never stopped to talk to us. Like many upper class civilians, he was "doing his bit" for the war effort. But there are limits, by Jove!

It should have been wonderful, but I was miserable and homesick. At the age of seven I suppose that was to be expected, despite being with my brother. Ironically, the lovely house, lawn, and servants made it all much worse. I was totally out of my element, and I wanted my scruffy old Liverpool back, bombs and all.

On the first visit my mother made, she realized that this was not working and applied for my brother and I to come home until a further evacuation home could be found. This would happen very soon after. We were placed on a bus with other evacuees and sent to a town in Wales, which was a long way from Liverpool (or so it seemed to me).

World War II evacuees boarding a train to the rural countryside in Great Britain, September 1939. © Alamy

When we arrived at the town square, other people were also arriving, assisted by government officials to pick up their charges. As time went by, the group thinned out considerably. When evening came, my brother and I were the only children left.

The government official turned to us and said, "We've made some calls. They'll be here soon."

We didn't know who "they" were, and I started to cry.

"Don't cry," said Stan.

"Why can't I cry?" I asked him.

"Because if you cry, I'll cry," my brother said, tearing up just a little. It is a routine that we have continued into adulthood and never fails to make us laugh.

Still, at the time it was not funny. A couple finally arrived and took us home. Our shared memory of the people and the house is extremely vague. However, we both remember that we did not get much to eat, and that very little attention was paid to us. Luckily, this unhappy experience did not last long. An evacuee inspector found that we were not getting the food and clothing that we needed, which the Government was paying for.

So, it was back to Liverpool again. But the bombing was still relentless, and our neighborhood was particularly hard hit so we could not stay. It was evacuation time again. We were sent to a small town called Rhos, near Wrexham in North Wales. We were to live with an older couple named Mr. and Mrs. Jones, the surname, of course, of everyone else in Wales.

It was third time lucky. They had no children of their own and they truly welcomed us. Kind and humorous, they even tried to teach us the Welsh language without much luck (though they had lots of fun trying). I also remember Mrs. Jones teaching me to pray for my family at home and kneeling with me by my bed.

Stan and I became part of the town life, even attending school in Rhos and mixing with the local children as well as other evacuees. Though it was difficult for her to get away, my mother paid the occasional visit and was happy to see us settled, at least for a time.

Eventually the bombing of cities stopped, and slowly the evacuees, including Stan and I, came home to live out the end of the war.

When the war was over, we kept in touch with Mr. and Mrs. Jones and even visited once or twice.

OUR BILL

B ill was my older brother but there was a period during the war years that he took on the role of father to my siblings and me. Even long afterwards I still tended to see him in that light.

Initially, my father had not been drafted into the armed forces when World War II started. With six children at the time and the only breadwinner, he was given a deferment. But inevitably, he was called up, not exactly to fight, but to serve in the Pioneer Corps, a battalion of laborers who did the heavy lifting and building at army bases around England. He was never posted abroad with fighting units, so we did not exactly have a war hero for a father. But we did have our dad alive and well at the end of the war, which unfortunately was not the case for some of the families around us.

When Dad went into the army, it left a huge gap, certainly financially. He did not earn much money, but it was a steady wage and paid the bills. Well, some of them anyway. My mother would now have to run the house and feed and clothe the family on just a meager Government Army allowance. Perhaps even more important than the money was the fact that my father was a loving husband, incredibly supportive of my mother who was very frail with a weak heart. He kept order in the house and was a bulwark against the demands and noise generated by six children living in a very small space. Now my mother would be left to deal with all this by herself.

My brother Bill, or "Our Bill," as he was called, a Northern England term for all relatives, had just left school. He was to take up an engineering apprenticeship with a local firm. This would alleviate the money problem somewhat, but not much since apprenticeship wages were extremely low.

Bill had always held a position of authority as the eldest son. But now he was really head of the family in every respect, despite being only seventeen years old.

The other siblings were as follows: Stan, who was fifteen, two years younger than Bill, myself age ten, Cyril age eight, Angela age six, and Dorothy age five. Our Bill's authority hardly came from his physique. Like most young working-class men at that time, he was small and slight— evidence of a poor diet and lack of proper nourishment. Like my mother he had those Welsh gypsy traits like his dark hair.

Within a very short time he started to put his stamp on the household. He organized the housekeeping jobs, some of which we had done before, but now our Bill had decided that we would do a lot more. In the early days under this new regime, I was on my hands and knees scrubbing the kitchen floor, feeling quite sorry for myself since the shouts of my mates playing soccer in the street could be heard just outside the backdoor.

I would ask my brother, "Bill, can I just clean this part and I promise to finish off after the game?"

"No, finish the floor and then you can go out to play."

"But they will be a player short if I don't go now."

In his bass, almost humorous tone he would say, "The longer you sit here arguing, the longer it will take to go out and play." It was that same voice that would eventually be crooning Perry Como and Bing Crosby songs around the house, when better times came.

Reluctantly, and probably with a theatrical sigh, my arms went back into the bucket of hot, soapy water, all the way up to the elbows.

That was our Bill—never shouting his authority, but quietly stating what he wanted done. If we were causing my mother stress by arguing or fighting with each other, he would step in to referee, and off we would go to our neutral corners. If one of us was intent on continuing to cause disruption, there was always the ultimate punishment of "The Coal Shed."

Every yard in the street had a small shed for delivery of coal for the house fire, which was the only source of heat in the house. The coal would be stacked and held in place by a section of wood. There was a door to the shed which could be locked from the outside.

When all else failed, the recalcitrant, screaming child would be carried and placed in the coal shed on top of the coal and the door would be locked. When the door closed, the screaming usually stopped and between quiet sobs there would be plaintive pleas to be let out and a heartfelt promise to be good for ever and ever, or something to that effect. I remember it well—the total darkness when the door closed and how frightened I felt. We were only kept there for minutes but they seemed like hours. My dad had started this very effective punishment and our Bill carried it on like some old and venerable family tradition. However, I seem to remember that he took a more humorous approach than my dad, handling it all with a smile on his face.

The first Christmas that my father was away was particularly difficult. My mother warned the older kids that there would be no money for presents. She told the little ones something to the effect of Father Christmas not being able to fly in the sky to bring gifts to the children because of the German bombers.

With that in mind, we awoke on Christmas morning expecting very little, if anything, in the way of gifts. However, upon going downstairs, I spotted something on the table. It was a fort that I had been asking for, with little hope of getting it, to go with my collection of toy soldiers. Alongside it was a toy tommy gun for my younger brother and two dollhouses for my sisters. Our Bill had made the toys at work where he had tools and a lathe. He kept the presents secret by hiding them in a back cupboard that no one used.

Thanks to our Bill it was a Christmas I will always remember.

Bill steered the family through to the end of the war, running interference for my mother by keeping us all in check and trying to make sure that we had enough money to see us through the week, though not always successfully.

With the end of the war and my father back home again, Bill was once again the eldest son, deferring to my father as head of the house. But in the eyes of his brothers and sisters, he would never lose the authority and respect he had earned over those difficult times when my father was away.

When happier times came, my father and mother would go out to the pub on weekend evenings. Our Bill and his pals, along with their girlfriends, would then come over to

our house. Among the gang would be Marjorie who soon after became his wife for over sixty years. The carpet would be rolled up for an evening of dancing and jiving to the American big band music of Count Basie, Glenn Miller, and Tommy Dorsey. The younger children would be sent to bed, but I was allowed a little more time with the adults.

Sometimes I would be asked to find a particular record, and wonder of wonders, put it on the turntable. The girls would make a fuss of me, and I was in heaven as I watched these attractive, happy people laughing and dancing the night away.

As my time to go to bed loomed nearer, I tried to make myself as inconspicuous as possible, hoping our Bill wouldn't notice that I was still around. But then inevitably I'd hear: "Hey, mate, bedtime. Up those wooden hills you go," and there was no arguing. So reluctantly, with the big band music as accompaniment, I trudged up the stairs to bed.

Goodnight, Bill!

THE ORANGE AND
THE GREEN

My father was an Orangeman – a fully paid up, card-carrying member of the Loyal Orange Lodge, an institution organized to promote Protestantism in Britain. At least, that was the stated aim of the organization.

Our family lived in an Irish Catholic area near the Liverpool docks. Next door to us were the Mallon's, then over the wall were the Tierney's, next to them the O'Brien's, and so on.

This is what made the whole "Orange" thing so bizarre because we were extremely friendly with all the neighbors. Their children were my friends, and on weekends my mother joined the women around us for Guinness and gossip at the pub at the end of the street. When a neighbor needed help in the form of a cup of sugar or a few shillings to get them through the week to payday, my mother would come to the rescue, if she could.

My father, however, did not interact with the neighbors unless it was absolutely necessary. He was prone to muttering anti-Catholic sentiments such as "They won't rest until everyone is Catholic," "They are all scared of Father Bunloaf," (the less than affectionate name for the local priest) and "They have kids just to get the family allowance."

The fact that he had seven children and never set foot in a church unless it was an Orange church parade seemed lost on him, even when the irony was pointed out (usually by me). A further irony is the fact that my father was a loving, gentle man, devoted to his wife and children and yet was still willing to air these prejudices. My mother would not confront him but would smile indulgently and usually would give us kids a wink on the side.

The children in our family were expected to join the juvenile branch of the Orange Lodge, attend meetings, and march in the parades on the Twelfth of July. It was the date celebrating the Battle of The Boyne, which was Protestant King William's victory over the Catholic King James. During the parade, bands would play and both children and adult members would march behind them through the neighborhood.

Many people came out to see the parades including friends of mine, both Protestant and Catholic, which embarrassed me to no end. Another aspect of these parades was their provocative nature. The Orange men and women marched through the Catholic areas with banners flying and drums beating in a triumphal procession of Protestantism. The Catholics resented it and tensions could get quite high, although I cannot remember any actual violence.

My siblings accepted all of this, but I balked continually, pleading with my father to let me leave the Orange Lodge since I believed none of it. This went on until I was around fourteen when my father agreed reluctantly to let me leave the Order. This decision hurt my father. He wanted more than anything for me to stay and eventually play an instrument in the band with my brothers. They did not necessarily embrace the Orange philosophy but went along for the sake of my father, and because they genuinely enjoyed playing in the band.

Two of them played the flute, one played the drum alongside my father, and the youngest, my brother Robert aged seven, was a mascot bandmaster marching in front of the official bandmaster to the "oohs" and "aahs" of the crowd. There was a certain glamour to the band since they dressed in military uniforms, and this was not lost on my brothers. Not only did it not have any appeal to me, but it could never make up for what the organization stood for.

After I left the Lodge, when it came to parades with the band, I was not averse to walking alongside my father. Being the lead drummer, he strode along in his smart uniform, and I couldn't help feeling so proud of him as I bathed in the reflected glory. I'm sure he wondered why I was happy to declare my affinity with the Orange Order at those times but not enough to actually commit to it.

The truth is, my father was in the Orange Lodge not from some deeply felt opinions about Protestant and Catholics, but simply because being in that uniform, playing that drum and leading that band gave him a stature and a presence that as a poor working-class laborer he would never otherwise have.

Our differences about the Orange Order never affected our relationship. He remained a loving, if undemonstrative, father until the day he died.

William Hughes Sr. (far right) drumming in the Orange Lodge parade celebrating the Battle of the Boyne on July 12th.

Garston True Blues, Loyal Orange Lodge - brother Cyril Hughes (back row, 5th from right), father William (Bill) Hughes Sr. (middle row, third from the left), brother Bill Hughes (middle row, far left)

AUNTIE LOU

It was 1944 in wartime Britain, and I was ten years old. My Auntie Louise was my mother's half-sister. She lived alone on the same street as our family, but in what was regarded the poorer end, next to the Tanning Yard and the entrance to the Garston Docks.

She would sit at her window for hours looking out at the people going by, making comments to no one in particular: "Look at Mrs. Kilgarry in a new coat with her kids running around barefoot!" or "Paddy Brady is off to the Vic again! I don't know where he gets the money to drink like that…"

Auntie Louise would walk over to our house regularly to have a cup of tea with my mother. She was a short, rather stout lady and we would watch her waddling up the street and over to our door.

"Auntie Lou's here, Mam! Will she read the tea leaves?"

One of the reasons we enjoyed her visits was because with very little persuasion, she would read the loose tea leaves at the bottom of the teacup for the three or four neighbors joining my mother for a morning cup of tea. She'd stare into someone's cup and point out some future happening in the leaves. It was all innocuous stuff, and if she saw some dire happening as foretold at the bottom of the cup, she would dramatically stop the proceedings by recoiling slightly from what she saw in the tea leaves, saying with a worried look on her face, "That's enough—I have to go now," leaving everyone, especially the person whose cup she was reading, in a certain state of anxiety. Years later, my mother would insist that Auntie Lou had been uncannily accurate and listed many of the events that came true.

However, the main reason that Auntie Lou was a favorite of mine was her love of the movies, or the "pictures" as we in Britain called them. There were two cinemas within walking distance of our house: the Empire and the Lyceum. There were two pictures every week that ran from Monday through Wednesday and Thursday through Saturday. In those days there were no showing on Sundays.

These two cinemas or "picture houses" had vastly different cultures. The Empire was the more sedate of the two, with a foyer housing a ticket window and marble steps leading into the cinema—very posh indeed. The Empire tended to show a classier type of picture, such as a Hollywood musical in Technicolor, a love story drama, and, inevitably, British comedies. There were two evening performances (called a First House and a Second House) and even a waiting room for the second house people.

The Lyceum, also known as "The Flea Pit," was a two mile walk from our house. The ticket window was almost on the street, with a tiny foyer for shelter. It was as shabby on the inside as it was on the outside. The carpeting initially welcomed you in but then gave way to concrete underfoot. As if with some sort of apology, it charged a little less than the Empire—10 pence as opposed to a shilling (12pence). The Lyceum tended to show a lower class of picture. "Charlie Chan the Chinese Detective" was a favorite, as were the Westerns.

This theater was also known for its raucous Saturday matinees when the kids ran amok, fighting with each other and pulling the hair of the girls in front, despite the efforts of the two harried usherettes in charge.

Auntie Lou was a frequent visitor to both of these picture houses, and she didn't care what picture was playing or whether it was any good. She just always tried to get to the pictures every Monday and Thursday. She did not like to go alone, and if a friend was not accompanying her, she would stop at our house and ask my mother if one of us would like to go with her. Since my other brothers and sisters were too young, it really came down to my older brother Stan or myself. So off we would go with Auntie Lou to see a movie for free.

From the time we started walking to the theater until the moment we got home, Auntie Lou rarely spoke a word. We might get "That was a good picture," but there was never a discussion, nor were there questions as to our reactions. We had been to the pictures, and that was that.

My evenings at the pictures with Auntie Lou were not my only access to the cinema and all its delights. If I saved enough money I would go alone or with a friend. We could go in to see a picture with a "U" for Universal rating without being accompanied by an adult. However, if the picture was rated "A," an adult companion was necessary. We worked around this by waiting outside the picture house until a friendly looking adult person, usually a genial couple on their way inside walked by.

"Could you take us in to the pictures, please?" If they agreed, we gave them our money and in we went. Sometimes we sat with them, but more often than not we would spot other friends using the same ruse and go join them.

My friends also liked the movies, but for all of us, scraping the money together to go was difficult. If one of us did manage to go, we were almost duty-bound to gather our friends around us and tell them the story of the movie and the characters in as great a detail as possible, sometimes even acting out the plot.

As Auntie Lou became more fragile and I became too old to be taken to the movies, our weekly jaunts came to an end. But a lifelong passion had been set in motion, thanks to her.

LET THE GAMES BEGIN

The front door of the house where I was born and raised was on King Street—Number 61A to be precise. But that front door was rarely used. It was our Victorian parlor for special occasions only. Our back door on Lucania Street was a different story. It opened onto a street that was the center of all the action for the neighborhood kids. It was where all the games were played.

It was 1945 and I was 11 years old. The war had just ended and a massive clean up was underway following the Blitz. The bombing attacks hit the city of Liverpool and my town of Garston particularly hard. Our close proximity to the docks hadn't helped. Thus finding a street where we could run and play was difficult indeed, and here we had one right outside our door.

On non-school days, or sometimes after school, my younger brother Cyril and I would take a tennis ball or similar rubber ball outside to kick around soccer style. Being born in Liverpool meant that soccer was a part of a boy's DNA and we were constantly honing our skills any way that we could.

Within a very short time other boys appeared, almost Pied Piper style, to join in the "kick around." Kenny Ellis arrived from the alleyway leading from his house. The Hill brothers, Les and Ray, made their entrance from nearby Shakespeare Street. Soon we had enough players for a five a side game.

The goal posts were the sewer grates on each side of the street. There was neither a coach nor a referee. All disputes were worked out among us quite amicably, probably because we just wanted to get on with the game.

The fact that we had to use a very small ball rather than a standard soccer ball (which we could not afford) actually helped in improving our soccer skills, especially with controlling the ball.

However, it was not all sunshine and roses. On each side of the street were the walls to two backyards. One was our house and if the ball went over our wall, it was quickly retrieved. But it was a different story with the other wall which belonged to the Gawn family house. If the ball went over Mrs. Gawn's wall (for some reason Mr. Gawn was never around) and was not quickly retrieved by one of us, she would keep it. The rule was that the person kicking a high ball over the wall had to scramble over quickly enough to beat Mrs. Gawn to the ball in her yard and scramble back, hopefully unscathed. I say that because Mrs. Gawn seemed to take a fiendish joy in attacking the interloper with her broom, so one had to jump over, grab the ball, and then jump back up, all the while evading the swinging weapon she was wielding.

"You're ruining my garden with that bloody ball so I'm keeping it!"

Actually, her garden consisted of a few scrawny plants but it was clear she intended to defend them to the death.

While the boys were enjoying our football (sorry, "soccer") and fighting off Mrs. Gawn's attacks, the girls in our street were playing games of their own. My two sisters, Angela and Dorothy, would be at the upper end of Lucania Street with a crowd of their friends playing hopscotch and swing rope games. On the corner of the street was a lamp post with two arms. The girls would throw ropes over the arms and swing around the lamp post at quite a speed...

The fact that the children were playing outside in the street was a godsend to their mothers. Their houses were too small and the families too big for the mothers to get all the cooking, cleaning, and various housework done. On those occasions when the weather was too bad to send the children outside, chaos reigned (and hijinks ensued).

In our house there were five children at home (my two brothers were away in the army), and we had to find ways to amuse themselves in a very small living room. The younger siblings would color or play with jigsaw puzzles, and though it began on a happy note, arguments would inevitably break out.

"Mam, our Angela's cheating on the puzzle! I'm not playing anymore!"

All the while, my younger brother Cyril and I (we were 18 months apart in age) were playing a game we invented that involved a ball and the flight of stairs. It started out happily enough, but soon I would be throwing the ball rather hard at him, bringing him to tears. Then before you know it we were wrestling furiously on the ground...

There would come a point my when my mother who was trying to get housework done and prepare my dad's dinner would be pushed to the limit and would look around for shoes and slippers. These were her weapons of choice when she was trying to bring some order to the household. As my brother and I were rolling around on the living room floor, the slippers and shoes would start to rain down on us.

"I'll kill the bloody lot of you! I'll hang for you lot, God forgive me!"

At this point we kids knew that our mother had reached a breaking point and it was time to make a hasty exit. The trouble was that we all decided to escape the combat zone at the same time, becoming squashed in the doorway together, making us an even easier target...

The irony of all this was the fact that my mother was the most cheerful, kind, fun loving person anyone could ever wish to meet.

That is, of course, until five children start playing indoor games...

**Northern England schoolchildren play football
in the street, 1946. © Alamy**

**Children find their own enjoyment with the aid
of a rope and a lamp post, 1943. © Alamy**

GINGER

Ginger appeared on the neighborhood scene later than the rest of the gang of boys who were my good friends. We all had attended kindergarten together, and then, later on, the local Protestant church school.

It was 1945 and The War (this was how we referred to it then and would forever after) had just ended. We were all around eleven years old.

Our gang played soccer in the street morning, noon and night, right outside the backdoor to my house. One day I saw a boy about our age whom I had never seen before, standing on the corner watching the game. During a break I asked that since we were a man short, would he like to join the game? He happily accepted and, although not highly skilled, he was useful enough on the team. He said his name was Billy Martin. He was of average height and his reddish ginger hair was slicked back. It didn't take long for him to be given the nickname "Ginger."

He told us that he and his father had recently moved from a district in downtown Liverpool which had been hit particularly hard by the bombing. The council had condemned these areas and relocated the families. I learned later that he was an only child, and that his mother had recently died of cancer.

He was a likable lad and immediately fit in with all of my main friends: Dava Jones, Bobby Whiteside, Frank

Yeadon, Big Pilly (Ray Hill) and Little Pilly (Les Hill), along with a supporting cast of dozens.

Ginger won us all over with his humor. He did hilarious imitations of radio stars, film stars and, later, of the teachers at the school we all attended. He could speak like Donald Duck and would lapse into his excellent imitation at the most inappropriate times. Hence his immediate popularity.

Before he arrived, I was the person in the group encouraging the gang when it came to seeking out fun and laughter in all kinds of situations. However, rather than resent his talent and popularity, I fed off his humor and he off mine and we became close friends. The years went by and as we entered our late teens, the gang remained together.

One of the golden opportunities for Ginger and me to perform was at the movies. Immediately after church on Sunday nights, our crowd would join the line waiting to see the "second house" or late show at the local Empire cinema. We knew almost everyone in line and spoke to neighborhood friends and also flirted with the girls.

We had to be very wary of the attendant Mr. Moore, who was always on the lookout for what he called "troublemakers." He would walk slowly up the line looking hard at the various groups. Mr. Moore had very flat feet which were at right angles to his legs, making him walk like a duck. This was tailor-made for Ginger to lapse into his Donald Duck routine as Mr. Moore went by. He would usually stop when he reached our group:

"We don't want any messing about when the picture starts. I've had trouble with you lot before."

We all put on our serious faces and I usually spoke up, offering assurance. "No, I don't think so Mr. Moore.

We haven't been here for a while and we're really looking forward to this picture."

I'm sure that I looked very earnest. I'm equally sure that Mr. Moore was not at all convinced.

If the movie was worthy of our attention, we would sit back and enjoy it. After all, we loved the movies. However, all too often it was some Hollywood clunker with cliché dialogue. The worst were the Cecil B. de Mille Biblical extravaganzas like "Sampson and Delilah." Of course, the more ridiculous the film, the more opportunity for Ginger and me to shout out our own dialogue to accompany the scene on the screen. We competed for the funniest, most outrageous lines to substitute those spoken in the movie. We had to have the audience with us, of course, and we usually did. It was our neighborhood crowd of young people we were at school with. They would be laughing in all the wrong places and inevitably Mr. Moore would soon be waddling down the stairs of the balcony area where we were sitting. He would shine his flashlight saying, "Any more noise and you will all be out!" We would sit with straight faces, supposedly engrossed in the action on the screen and acting just a little startled by his noisy intrusion.

Another one of our escapades involved Ginger and I singing in the choir. We were both in the school chorus at Heath Road School, and at practice he would place himself in the line directly behind me. We would launch into something from a Gilbert and Sullivan operetta with gusto, when suddenly Ginger would lapse into singing in his Donald Duck voice. For some reason this didn't seem to affect anyone around him. Perhaps they thought that it was his normal voice. But I, however, was convulsing and could not stop laughing no matter how hard I tried.

"Stop, Stop!"

That was Mr. Parker, the Chorus Master.

"Hughes seems to be enjoying this far more than the rest of us. Pray tell us why, so that we may all join in the fun."

"Sorry, sir, fit of the giggles."

Mr. Parker would then pull me out of the group for a while. Ginger, of course, would act the soul of innocence as though nothing had happened.

I soon learned that Ginger was determined never to take anything particularly seriously. He thought that people were ridiculous, and that life was absurd. Or was it the other way around? Anyway, why not just sit back and enjoy the fun?

6th Allerton Scouts Football Club, Garston, Liverpool: Ginger Martin (front row, 2nd player from left–hands on knees), Derek (front row, 2nd player from right–arms crossed).

This is where we parted ways philosophically. Yes, I wanted mischief and fun wherever I could find it, but I also had other interests. I loved sports and took them very seriously. I went to a fine school, so academics were an important part of my life, and as I got older, I enjoyed girls, unlike Ginger.

Ginger was not interested in girls and did not set out to impress them when they joined us in the street, in the movies, or at the dance. As long as he had his male friends and as long as he was able to go for a pint and a laugh, he was happy.

Inevitably, some of us began taking girls out on dates, and despite the fact that we still met up at the dance or at the pub, soon that old gang of mine was breaking up.

The National Service was also a factor. We were all called to serve the mandatory two years at the age of eighteen in one of the services. Most of my friends went into the Army, and I was in the Royal Air Force. Ginger opted for five years in the Royal Navy to get the better pay.

He was to return a changed man, but that's a story for a little later on.

SATURDAY MORNING AT GRAN'S

I was about twelve years old when I was told by my parents that on Saturday mornings I was to go to my Grandmother's house to run her errands. This was something that had been done by both my older brothers until they left school and started work.

I was quite happy about it. I had always enjoyed going to my Gran's since I was a small boy, and since my Saturday soccer game was in the afternoon, I had no problem with running her "messages" (the local word for errands). So off I went at 8:30 in the morning on the twenty minute walk to my Gran's house. My route took me along King Street,

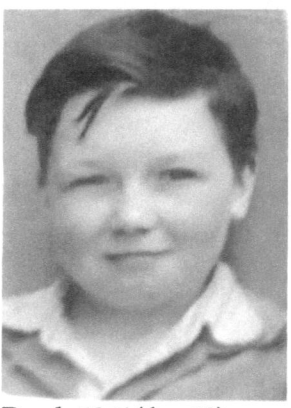

Derek, 1946 (Age 12)

where I lived, under the railway bridge and then up the "Brew," the steep road that took me to Clifton Street where my Grandmother lived.

I knocked on the door of Number 48 and could hear Gran shuffling down the small corridor from her living room. She opened the door and gave me that quiet smile that she always seemed to have. "Hello love, come on in, I'm just about to make a cup of tea." This was hardly surprising. Gran was always either making a cup of tea, drinking a cup of tea, or had just finished one.

She was wearing her standard uniform of a long house dress down to her ankles, with a cardigan over it. She had on a pair of slippers. She was a thin, slight woman and wore her hair in a bun. She would not have looked out of place in a Victorian photograph.

We both sat in the small living room which had a table, chairs and a tiny settee next to a small grate for a fire. Off the living room was the back kitchen, although I never understood the term because there was no front kitchen. The only other room downstairs was the parlor which nobody ever used. In those old houses the parlor was for "special" company. I have to assume that this meant royalty because I can never remember ever seeing anyone in the family, or even visitors, using it.

Gran lived in the house with my grandad and my Uncle Leslie, her only bachelor son. Her two other sons, which included my father, and her three daughters were all married with their own homes.

Gran was not at all talkative, but we could sit quietly together without strain. I might read one of my comics or a schoolbook, and now and again Gran would ask a question about someone in the family.

Then it was time for the errands. Gran did not give them to me all at once. She had her own system where she gave me one errand at a time. When I returned, she would make some tea and then she would give me the list for the next errand. I like to believe that she did this, not because she had no faith in my ability to handle the multiple instructions, but because she enjoyed my company and liked to prolong our time together.

The shops were all nearby: the Chinese laundry, the greengrocer, the grocery shop, the tobacconist and most important of all, The Chippie—the fish and chip shop, always the culmination of my shopping morning.

And so off I went, in and out of the house on various errands with the clock inching toward the bewitching noon hour. At twelve o'clock the factory sirens would blare out the end of the work week and the gates of the Nuts and Raisin factory, the Matchworks, the Bobbinworks, the Silkworks, the Bottle Works and the Garston Docks, would all open and the workers would pour out with their wages in their pockets, ready to enjoy the weekend.

Meanwhile at Number 48 Clifton Street, Gran and I were preparing the last and the most important errand of the day—Le Grand Fish and Chip order, which was the lunch for all the workers in the family. It was very important that I get this right, so I wrote the orders down myself as Gran peered anxiously over my shoulder.

"Two fish for Grandad, and don't forget the mushy peas," she said. Then down the list for Auntie Brenda, Auntie Dolly, and Uncle Les. (He was fishcake—no fish.) There was, of course, chips with everything.

Gran never ordered anything herself. In fact, I cannot recall ever seeing her eat anything because she was always too busy looking after everybody else.

Atkins Chip Shop was just around the corner so the orders would still be hot when I brought them back. As I waited for my turn in the small queue, I watched Mr. Atkin place large potatoes in the "chipper" at an alarming speed. Down he would press on the handle and a number of chipped potatoes would fall into the large pan. These would then be heaved into a huge bowl of fat with a net pan to lift the hot, steaming chips onto the greaseproof paper, then newspapers would be laid out on the counter. Mrs. Atkins would then roll up the orders at the end of this rather short but effective assembly line. I would pack the orders into my shopping bag and run out of the shop. There was no time to waste.

No sooner had I given the bag to Gran to sort out than the front door would open, and my two aunts would arrive. Auntie Dolly who worked at the local greengrocers, and Auntie Brenda who worked at the Nuts and Raisin factory, would breeze in, laughing uproariously at something or other. They would then be followed by a more subdued Uncle Leslie who was employed at the Silk Works. My aunts were both buxom ladies with round, cheerful faces. Uncle Les was a quiet man who found it difficult to keep up with his more energetic sisters.

"Hello, luv, I hope you got the chips in, I'm starving!" Auntie Brenda would say, speaking for everyone.

The next entrance would be the somber arrival of my grandad, who would walk in from his morning on the docks. He would pick up his newspaper and sit in his armchair waiting for Gran to bring his meal and anything else he wanted. He might give me a curt nod but, then again, he might not.

During the meal my aunts would talk and laugh constantly, sometimes pushing each other to emphasize the humor as my Uncle Les joined in the joke occasionally. I would sit in the corner quietly, observing it all. Sometimes one of my aunts would come running over and clamp their hands over my ears saying, "You're too young for this kind of talk!"

Sometimes I would catch Gran's eye and she would give me that smile which said "Aren't they outrageous? And isn't this wonderful?" I totally agreed on both counts.

At the end of the meal, Grandad would stand up, tuck his newspaper under his arm and announce, "I'm going down the yard." He would then stride out of the door and down to the lavatory halfway down the back yard. No one paid much attention and the loud, raucous conversation would continue.

Quite often on these Saturday mornings, my father would stop in to see his parents and say hello to his family. He was my Gran's favorite, and when she saw him walking up the yard her face would light up, saying "Oh, here's our Bill!" as though it was some wonderful surprise. No one would ever guess that she had seen him just two days earlier.

My dad and I would leave together to go home, but not before my Gran, aunts and uncle had each quietly given me some money as a thank you for my help during the morning. They had no idea that I would have paid them for the privilege.

PART 2

A Drinking Life

In my neighborhood of Liverpool, England during World War II, drinking was as natural as breathing. On weekends, the pubs would be packed with men chugging their pints and women sipping their bottles of Guinness Irish stout, all paid for with money they could ill afford. However, to people whose lives were not only bleak, but at times dangerous from never knowing when the next air raid would take place, it was an outlet they desperately needed.

Many of the men were away in the armed forces. Some of those left behind were the dockers loading and unloading the ships coming in and out of the Liverpool port, a prime target for the German bombers that flew over, sometimes on a nightly basis. People felt that if their house wasn't hit on the last air raid, it was a cause for celebration. "Let's Have Another One" was the title of a popular song at the time and people took it literally.

Many of the women, with their husbands away, had to live on a small government allowance out of which they had to feed and clothe their usually large families. At night came the air raids, and the herding of the children to safety in air raid shelters. It was difficult, stressful, and dangerous. It was no wonder that people would save their pennies during the week in order to have a drink at the weekend. The good news was that there was certainly no lack of choice when it came to going to the pub.

We lived on King Street. As you entered the street you saw the first pub on the corner, called the Cock and Trumpet. It was only a hundred yards from the Garston Dock gates and was a favorite with the dockers, especially on pay day. Many of those workers would drink their wages away before they even got home.

Walking on for a few hundred yards brought you to McGarry's aka The King's Vaults, which was my Mum's local. On weekends she would meet her friends from the neighborhood for a drink and a gossip. If you walked a little further, you'd see the "Vic," aka the Victoria, on another corner. And that was just our street alone. On the streets around it, standing on each corner like battlements surrounding a fortress, were the Raglan, the Canterbury, the Woodcutters Men's Club, and the Clarence.

These public houses ranged from the very shabby, drab, and dark with sawdust on the floor, to the well-lit, many-mirrored establishments. However, people did not go to the pub for the architecture. They usually went to the one nearest to them, or their "local," as it was called, where they could meet up with people from their street. Upon entering, there would be a Men's Bar for men only, and then The Parlour, which was for both men and women. Some of the pubs had a window opening on the street, called the "Off License," where people could bring jugs to be filled with beer to be taken home to family who were not able to get out.

The only reason for going to other pubs away from the neighborhood was when the young men, almost as a rite of passage, went on a "pub crawl." This meant having a drink in as many different pubs as possible before succumbing and having to be escorted home by their mates.

My mother would sit and count the money in her purse.

"Do you have any money, love? Maggie (aka Mrs. Butler, our next door neighbor) said she would meet me in McGarry's for a Guinness, and I'm a bit short."

I worked at the local butcher's shop on Saturdays and although I turned over the few shillings I received to my mother, she would give me something back as pocket money. So I gave her what I had, which was more than enough for a bottle of stout.

"Thanks love, I'll see you straight on Saturday. It's been a bloody awful week. I'll go mad if I don't get out for an hour."

A bottle of stout, a cigarette, a laugh, a good "natter" with friends, and maybe a song or two—that was therapy for the women like my mother, with lots of children, a husband away in the forces, very little money, and bombs dropping, almost on a nightly basis.

There was a darker side to this drinking culture. Some of the men drank their wages away and came home in a rage and took it out on their wives and children. Our neighbor would sometimes appear at our door crying with bruises on her face, asking for my mother. We would be shooed out of the house while my mother comforted her, keeping her there until the husband calmed down.

There were also fistfights on Saturday nights outside some of the pubs. We kids loved it and news of a fight spread like wildfire.

"I just heard there's a big punch-up outside the Vic between the Moran's and the Doyle's!" one of my friends would report breathlessly. We would then run as fast as we could to the fracas.

For the most part, however, the drinking that I observed, certainly in my house, was something positive.

After the war when my father came home, and money became more plentiful, he and my mother would go out to the pub on weekends with other couples. My favorite couple was my Auntie Nell, Mum's sister, and her husband Charlie. My mother and Auntie Nell were extremely close. They had been in service together as maids in a large house outside of Liverpool before they both married. They were a lively couple. They would come back to our house when the pubs closed, bringing back a few bottles of beer and continuing the party. They knew all of the old music hall songs as well as a dance or two, and they would perform for us in our tiny living room.

Watching my father and Uncle Charlie was also part of the show. They were a complete contrast to their wives. Dad would sit with a slight smile on his face, shaking his head from time to time. He did not drink much but he enjoyed watching my mother have fun.

Bill and Aggie Hughes

"Come on, Bill, you know this one!" my mother would say as she reached out to pull him up. Dad adored my mother, but wild horses couldn't drag him to join in her performance.

"Bugger off!" he would say with a smile, pulling away.

Uncle Charlie usually showed total indifference and would read the paper or talk to Dad. We kids loved it all and just tried not to be noticed in case we were sent to bed and missed the rest of the fun.

Many of the pubs in my hometown of Garston have now closed down. I will always remember them as a sort of secret weapon, helping people to endure those very difficult wartime years.

Schooldays

The year was 1947 and I was thirteen years old. I was sitting in class at Gilmour Secondary Modern School when suddenly the door opened, and the headmaster's secretary came into the room. She went over to the teacher, whispered something to him, and then left.

My teacher then looked at me and said, "Hughes, Mr. Simpson wants you in his study right away."

This was not good. Usually, a summons to our headmaster Ronald Simpson meant only one thing—punishment, usually in the form of bending over to receive six lashes across the behind with a cane.

Mr. Simpson was known for wandering the halls of the school, dragging his unfortunate impediment of a clubfoot behind him like some malevolent character in a horror movie. He made a point of looking for boys who had been sent out of class for misbehaving. He would then take them back to his study for a tongue lashing, if they were lucky, or a caning if they were not.

I searched desperately in my mind for the reason behind my being summoned. Had a teacher complained about me? Perhaps I was not the best-behaved pupil at Gilmour and I could be somewhat disruptive at times, but this only led to mild annoyance from the teachers since my schoolwork was more than satisfactory.

By the time I turned all of this over in my mind I was at Simpson's door. I knocked, and when I was called in, I was surprised to see two other boys, Jimmy Percival and Eric Addison, both of whom I knew well, standing in front of the headmaster's desk.

"Good, good, now you are all here." Mr. Simpson was actually smiling. My whole being gave a sigh of relief, especially my rear end.

"I am very pleased to tell you all that the scholarship results are in, and you three boys have all won places at Liverpool Institute High School for Boys." He then went on about our school being very proud, etc. and then said, "I understand, Hughes, that you only managed to scrape by, so I hope you will work extra hard."

"Well, thank you very much, sir. That's just the kind of humiliating encouragement I needed, especially in front of my scholarship co-winners." Actually, I didn't exactly say that, but I wish I had.

Simpson finished up the meeting by saying, "You have all done very well and I want you to take the rest of the day off. Now go home and tell your families the good news."

I did indeed race home. My joy gave me wings as I dashed out of school and ran the two miles all the way to my house. I burst through the door to find my mother sitting in her chair by the fire, drinking a cup of tea and smoking a Woodbine cigarette. Unable to wait one moment longer to share my exciting news I blurted out, "Mam! Mam! I won the scholarship!"

She didn't hug me or cry, or say how clever I was. My mother merely smiled at me, looking quite tired, and said, "Oh, that's nice love."

She then went on to say, "Now I'm glad you're home early. I need you to go to the shops and get something for Dad's tea…"

As I look back on this, I am surprised that in retrospect I was not crushed or even disappointed at what to modern day ears would seem to be a rather cool reception, requiring at least a year's therapy. However, I was not fazed at all because her reaction made all the sense in the world.

She did not really understand what the scholarship meant, and had far more important things on her mind. This was simply the way that people expressed themselves in our working-class milieu—curb that emotion, hold that enthusiasm… and I understood that.

Yet I knew my mother was pleased by the news, and proud of me. In those words and that smile she spoke loving volumes.

My six siblings had various reactions, from teasing me for going to a posh school to general indifference. The Liverpool Institute High School for Boys was an elite high school with a history going back a 100 years. It has many distinguished alumni, or "Old Liobians," Sir Paul McCartney and George Harrison being among them. It was only in the 1940's that such schools allowed scholarship pupils to attend. Before that, the English class system prevailed, and only the sons of gentlemen were permitted—for a price. The academic curriculum was quite rigorous, with an emphasis on Latin and Greek in certain advanced classes. Not surprisingly, that did not include mine.

It was not exactly "Tom Brown's Schooldays" but you get the idea. There was homework, lots of it, as well as tests and exams. It was quite different from the easygoing curriculum at Gilmour and the council education system in general.

My new school was not all good news. For one thing, it imposed a financial burden on the family. There was a strict dress code for the school uniform which was the required blue blazer with grey pants, white shirt, green and black school tie, and a badge worn on the blazer with the Latin school motto "Non nobis solem sed toti mundo nati" which means "Not for ourselves alone, but for the whole world."

There was also the ever-present school cap. Woe betide any boy caught not wearing it within a mile of the school. Some of the boys even had more than one school uniform. My parents had help from a government grant, but it was still difficult for them. I had to wear the same one and tried to keep it somewhat respectable throughout the long school term which included many a school yard soccer game.

And so my school year began. At first, I struggled, along with the other scholarship boys, to keep up with the homework, which was something I was not at all used to. It didn't help that outside of my window, as I tried to tackle a math problem or a German translation, I could hear the shouts of my friends playing in the street.

It was not as though my parents insisted on my

JOHN MANNERS LTD.
Specialist in BOYS WEAR
are stockists of complete School uniform for
LIVERPOOL INSTITUTE HIGH SCHOOL
and many other good schools on Merseyside

Extended payments now available on our
BUDGET ACCOUNT SERVICE
Ask for details from your nearest branch
5/7/9, Renshaw Street, Liverpool, 1
21, Basnett Street, Liverpool, 1
Tel: ROYal 3096.

doing my homework and studies. They took very little interest in my schooling and left everything to me. It was my choice whether I studied or not. They had many other things on their minds, like my father keeping his job as a laborer in order to feed a family of nine, for instance.

It was all very strange and intimidating at first. But eventually I came to enjoy the rituals and traditions of this well-known school. The morning assembly, for instance, was almost a church service. We sang hymns and listened to the scripture—no separation of church and state here.

The teachers were called "masters" and classes were "forms" as in Lower 5C. I was Hughes of Upper 4D. Come to think of it, there was something of a "Tom Brown's Schooldays" quality to it after all.

The masters wore armless, black gowns and would stride along the school corridors with their gowns billowing behind them, looking like large blackbirds with their wings outstretched.

The real aim of schools like Liverpool Institute was to prepare boys for a university education, and a portion of the pupils from affluent families took that route. For boys like me, that was an extremely difficult path to choose. The university education was free, but attending was expensive. There was no way that my parents would have been able to manage it. The choice I made was to take my finals and leave for a much better career than I could have managed with a council education. In any case, my academic performance was middling at best and even with funds, a place at a university would have been a real stretch.

Then there was a third option. At the age of sixteen boys were allowed to leave school, forgo their final exams, and find a job. After three years of rigorous school work and watching your mates earn money, it was a real temptation for me. However, it meant looking for work without a diploma from a prestigious school, and those years of hard work at school would be lost. Still, many boys from poor families did it. In fact, the two boys from Gilmour, Eric Addison and Jimmy Percival, both left Liverpool Institute and found a job.

I was now firmly ensconced in the life of the school and although hardly one of the star pupils, I was reading the classics, studying Shakespeare, singing Gilbert and Sullivan, and playing football and cricket for the school teams.

In my street life I still socialized with my same group of friends who all attended council schools. They left school at fifteen and usually became blue collar workers at the apprentice level. For the most part they were all bright, intelligent people, but because of the selective program of education in the UK they were "streamed" into schools which could not maximize their potential. And so was lost an enormous amount of talent.

It made me especially grateful to be a scholarship boy in Liverpool in the 1940's. I was on my way.....

Columned front entrance to Liverpool Institute

Wrought iron gates and dual spiral staircases lead up to the gallery of the
Main Hall, a horseshoe-shaped amphitheater

My First Job

I walked into the living room of our house, greeted by my mother who was, as usual, sitting in a chair by the unlit fire place, smoking a Woodbine cigarette with a cup of tea beside her. Her usual smile beamed out.

"Hello, love, you've just missed the vicar, he was looking for you."

"What did he want?" I asked.

"He was wondering what your plans were for a job now that you've left school."

I was seventeen years old and had just finished my schooling.

"Anyway, he said that he will look for you after church on Sunday."

Canon Lindsay, Vicar of Garston Parish Church, was a rather intense, fussy little man, with absolutely the best of intentions which, considering his calling, was certainly appropriate.

He had taken a special interest in me ever since I had won the scholarship. Young members of his congregation attending schools like the Liverpool Institute were few and far between, if any. He would enquire about the subjects I was studying and my exam results at the end of term. So from time to time I received a "Well done, Derek," or perhaps more often, "Never mind, better luck next time."

Although neither my mother nor my father attended church, they insisted on their children going to Sunday School and Junior Church services. One by one as they grew older, my siblings stopped attending, but I continued. My friends and I became part of the social group at church. This meant meeting girls our age, a good reason to continue our churchgoing. As part of my leaving exams, I studied the subject "Scripture Knowledge" and passed the exam. This was sufficient reason, I suppose, for the local vicar to take an interest in my progress. Now that my schooling was over, he seemed determined that I not take the path of most of the boys my age.

My friends in the neighborhood had left school at fifteen, having attended local schools without the rigorous academic standards demanded by the scholarship schools which prepared students for University (if they could afford it).

Manufacturing jobs were plentiful. It was the early 1950's and Britain was rebuilding after the devastation of World War II. The streets around us were ringed with factories: the Tannery Works, the Bottle Works, the Bobbin Works, Morton's Engineering, the Matchworks factory, and of course, Garston Docks, part of the Liverpool dock complex which dominated the riverfront just a short distance from our homes. There was no shortage of work in this area, that's for sure. But it was not the kind of work I wanted, and luckily Canon Lindsay seemed to feel the same way.

After Church on Sunday the vicar pulled me aside and told me that he had arranged an interview for me with the Branch Manager of the local Westminster (later, the National Westminster) bank. He knew the bank manager through the Rotary Club and became aware that a position had opened up for an office clerk, since the young woman in that job (unusual in those days) was leaving to get married.

The day for the interview arrived and I was incredibly nervous. I was venturing out from my universe of lower working-class into the world of the "posh" people, who thought, spoke, dressed, and acted quite differently than us.

I did not have a suit, but I did wear a jacket and tie and looked fairly presentable, or so I thought anyway. I met with the manager, Mr. Arthur Rowland, in his office. He was a large man physically, and rather pompous.

He started off by saying, "You understand, Mr. Hughes, (I looked around for Mr. Hughes, then realized that it was me) that normally we would advertise this position and interview a number of candidates. However, the vicar speaks very highly of you, and considering both your schooling and record I suppose we could give it a try."

Not the most enthusiastic welcome to an employee but looking back I realize that this was a type of affirmative action before its time. Obviously, Canon Lindsay must have pressed hard on the question of giving a local boy from a poor neighborhood a chance.

We talked vaguely about my duties which would be given to me in more detail when I started work. Then suddenly, the interview was over. I had the job, and though it was given rather reluctantly, I nevertheless secured the position.

Mr. Rowland stood up and towered over me. It felt like something out of a Charles Dickens novel, with the powerful authority figure staring down at the street urchin. He then ended the interview with a parting shot.

"You do realize that you will need a suit for the office?" he asked.

"Yes sir, I am aware of that," I stammered.

At home the news caused quite a stir. Our Derek had a job in a bank and would be going to work in a suit and tie. Just wait until the neighbors hear this! Even my mother, who was as self-effacing and modest a person as you would ever find, had a little swagger in her step when she went to meet the ladies at the local pub for their Guinness, gossip, and cigarettes.

There were also the jokes along the lines of, "Will you be bringing work (meaning cash) home?" "We'll never be short of money now, will we?"

Even the butcher I worked for on Saturdays got into the act. He would say to an array of customers, "Well ladies, Derek here has been very clever and will be working for the Westminster Bank. How do you like that?" This was met with a chorus of "Oooooh..."

I beamed proudly through it all but inwardly I was petrified. My interview with Mr. Rowland had given me some indication of what I would be facing. How would I know what to do? I would be entering a whole new world totally alien to everything I had experienced. Even at the Liverpool Institute I had mixed only with boys of my own kind, and I avoided, as much as I could, the boys from the posh parts of Liverpool.

The English class system is relentless in its quest to put its stamp on everyone, letting them know where they belong, and don't you forget it. Who did I think I was working in a bank? Getting a little above myself perhaps, as I am sure some of the neighbors sniffed to each other.

The day came when I had to report for work at the bank. I had a new suit and shirt. My father had shined my shoes until you could see your face in them. This made me feel better, but I was still tense about the day ahead.

It did not take long to become familiar with my duties at the bank. They were hardly taxing. We were a small local branch with a staff of eight plus our manager, Mr Rowland. My work involved sorting checks, balancing ledgers, answering the phone, and making tea.

Oddly enough, my biggest challenge was the telephone. No one in our neighborhood had their own phone. My only contact with a phone was through the red phone box on every corner for the occasional emergency call. Consequently, when the phone rang, I was actually afraid to answer it. When I did, in my nervousness, I failed to hear people correctly and usually got the message wrong. Sometimes it would ring and ring and I would pretend not to hear it until someone inevitably shouted, "Would someone answer that damn phone?" Over time I conquered this dread, but it did lead to some uncomfortable moments.

It was an all-male staff except for the woman I was replacing. My colleagues were nice enough, but they had nothing at all in common with me. They all owned their semi-detached homes with a garden, courtesy of the bank's very low employee mortgage rate. Most of the staff had their own car, which was quite a luxury in the 1950's. They dressed in well-pressed suits with crisp white shirts, and some of the older men, probably following Mr. Rowland's example, even had stiff detachable collars, which I thought had gone out of fashion when Queen Victoria died.

We all addressed each other as "Mr." unless it was during a tea break and then first names were allowed.

Even then there were no Charlie's, Alfie's or Jimmy's—it was always Charles, Alfred, or James. They talked about their weekend golf or tennis game, or perhaps a wonderful afternoon tea with neighbors, all of which was totally outside my experience. They politely asked about my weekend which was all about playing football, being with friends and going to the dance. Why was I so embarrassed about that? However, I slowly began to feel their acceptance and to feel more comfortable in the office. I was actually beginning to believe that I belonged.

My fears, stoked by class resentment, had proved groundless. I was not treated as an outsider—my fellow workers were friendly and helpful. It seems that I had treated myself as the outsider.

After eighteen months I was in the Royal Air Force doing my two year National Service. I would return to the bank since the law required that employers keep those jobs open, but that is another story entirely...

ON PARADE

"Left Right! Left Right! Left Wheel! About Turn! Squadron, halt!"

The not so dulcet tones of Corporal McCormick rang out over the parade ground of the Royal Air Force base in Celle, Germany. My squadron, NO. 17 RAF Regiment was being put through its paces, as it was every morning before we went to our work on the anti-aircraft guns.

But today was different. We had been out here for nearly two hours, an hour longer than usual and it wasn't difficult to understand why. Corporal McCormick had only recently been promoted from the ranks and he was playing with his newfound authority like a child with a new toy. He could make over a hundred men move, turn, stop, and run, all just by barking an order—it was that simple. Omnipotence had never felt so good to our dear beloved Corporal, and he was determined to make the most of it.

The year was 1954 and the squadron was a group of 18-20 year olds who were drafted into the Royal Air Force under the National Service Act of England. Rather than embracing the service as a career, we mildly resented this intrusion into our lives, and people like McCormick certainly didn't help.

It was very cold, and the mutterings and cursing began to grow in intensity all around me. Then came the last straw. Just as we were marching off the parade ground to the warmth of the gun sheds and a tea break before work, we suddenly heard "About turn!" We couldn't believe it —we were back on parade. And then...

"McCormick, you're a fucking idiot!"

The words that formed this epithet, this obscenity, seemed to

Derek (center) with RAF squadron, 1954

float over the parade ground for what felt like an eternity. Everybody froze, afraid to move even a muscle.

I was the one who had shouted. In a moment of stupidity, I had given vent to the frustration that everyone was feeling, as though somehow I had been elected spokesman for the squadron. I hadn't, of course, and although I probably had their admiration for saying what everyone thought, I was alone on this one.

Corporal McCormick came striding over to the ranks of men standing very stiffly to attention, more from tension than discipline.

"Step forward, the airman who shouted that remark!"

Not especially good grammar and there wasn't even a "please," but under the circumstances I decided to let that pass.

For a moment I contemplated the coward's way out by remaining silent. But I realized that this could make things very difficult for my mates, and McCormick would find out anyway. Sooo... I stepped forward out of the ranks, stamping my heels together very smartly with a "One-Two!" in real RAF Regiment style—nothing sheepish or apologetic about that...

Despite my bravado, as I was marched away with an escort to the military police barracks, the full import of what I had done began to sink in. My action wasn't exactly "Mutiny on the Bounty" material, but it was very serious and could possibly mean a court martial offense. My immediate fate was in the hands of Squadron Leader Hamilton who was the senior officer on base and I was soon in his office for a hearing. He sat at his desk flanked by two M.P.'s.

If I was a little uncertain regarding my predicament, Squadron Leader Hamilton clarified the situation and elaborated on how insubordination was one of the most serious of military offenses, that it strikes at the heart of all discipline, that the services could not function if orders were disobeyed, officers would be held up to ridicule, and so forth. I still could not believe that this was happening to me. It was like some out of body experience, but I tried to focus and to listen intently.

As Hamilton continued, I began to wonder, did I detect a "However" hovering somewhere in his recitation? Surely not. "But then, wham!" It arrived like the cavalry to my rescue.

"*However*, this is your first offense and I have also taken into account other mitigating factors. You are very active in squadron activities." Obviously, he meant that I was captain of the squadron soccer team, which was doing very well, thank you very much. "I note that you also assist Warrant Officer Harvey in his duties." "Bunny" Harvey was responsible for soccer and I filed papers, drank tea, and talked soccer with him in his warm, cozy office.

"I should also mention that Corporal McCormick has also put in a good word for you," continued Hamilton. What? Now this I could not believe. McCormick? We moved in different circles, and I hardly knew the man, even before he was promoted to corporal. However, he was an editor on the camp newspaper, and I had written something for it. I also vaguely remember discussing some ideas with him. Perhaps that was it. Maybe he was a decent chap after all... besides being a fucking idiot, I mean.

I was sentenced to two weeks in the base cells and work detail wherever needed in the camp. The offense would not appear on my record since I had gone no further than the preliminary hearing, and therefore no court martial. I was a lucky man, indeed.

Now came the serving of my time.

I had been sentenced to fourteen days in the military police barracks at the camp base and had no idea what I would be facing.

To my fellow airmen and myself, the camp guard house where I would be housed was the concrete structure with the barred windows high in the walls that we passed on our way into town on our furlough days. It was manned by a staff of military police always looking extra smart in their RAF uniforms with white belts and white gators around their ankles. They also looked rather intimidating and were invariably unsmiling and unfriendly. We were never sure if this was real or just an act forced upon them by RAF Central Casting. Anyway, we preferred to give them a wide berth and avoided contact if we possibly could. This was the guard house where I was taken after my hearing with the Squadron Leader.

I was processed into custody by an MP who continued to stay in character—the rough, tough cop. The premises were far less imposing on the inside. A desk and files for the M.P.'s, then a few steps down to a row of six cells along the wall.

I was taken to a cell and had just sat down on the bed to take in my surroundings when the door burst open and two men came running in. One of them held me down whilst the other grabbed my boots and began tying up the laces. They left as quickly as they had arrived. Before I could check on what had happened, I heard, "Cell inspection! Prisoners, stand by your beds!"

A very young officer carrying a baton walked through my cell door, followed by a much older flight sergeant. The routine was for the officer to walk around the cell, with the prisoner behind, and the flight sergeant bringing up the rear. The bed, blankets, and pillow had to be squared away in accordance with regulations, and the room had to be clean with no dust anywhere. The officer walked ahead, poking with his baton and using white gloves to check for dust.

However, as I followed the officer, I realized that my two assailants had tied my laces together so that I could not walk. This meant that to keep up, I had to make jack rabbit jumps to move me along. The officer kept giving nervous glances over his shoulder wondering perhaps, in his inexperience, whether this was the way all cell inspections were made, and that perhaps the prisoners did jumping jacks as part of the routine.

Not so, apparently, because the flight sergeant kept hissing in my ear as I hopped along, "I will see you later, and I will get you for this, airman." Actually, he never did pursue the issue, probably putting two and two together. As soon as inspection was over and they had left, my fellow inmates appeared again. They were roaring with laughter at the predicament they had placed me in but most of all they were happy that I had not "ratted" on them.

They were both in custody for the same crime, having beaten up German nationals in the town. This was very much frowned upon by the Occupation authorities, and of course, the German nationals weren't too happy either. My new friends constantly spoke about the irony of the situation in that they faced a court martial for beating up Germans, but ten years ago they might have received a medal for doing the exact same thing. Somehow, they found it impossible to see the difference between the two sets of circumstances.

It was not their first offense, and both had in fact been in trouble throughout their RAF careers. They were not National Service men, but "regulars" having signed up for five years or more, not because they saw the RAF as a career, but because they had nothing in "Civvy Street" and the money was better as a volunteer.

During my time with them they guided me through the guardhouse routine, discussing the various policemen on duty and how to handle them. On that score I found that for the most part the police dropped the tough persona once they were inside the guard house and certainly when they realized that a prisoner would not cause trouble.

Despite their problems my cell mates were full of fun and made my time there so much easier. Nevertheless, the court martial and its aftermath loomed large, but they refused to talk about it, and lived in the present.

Life as a prisoner on base was more boring than punitive. The MP's had to find work for us to do around camp and we would hang around waiting to see where we would be going. Was it the base gardens, digging and hauling plants? Or the cookhouse, moving garbage, peeling potatoes, or would we be cleaning up around the camp generally? It was all rather bland, nothing too uncomfortable or difficult. Wherever I went I inevitably ran into my mates from the squadron and received all the gossip and rumors of the day.

When work detail was over, we lounged around our cells playing cards, sometimes with the MP's, and writing letters. Alacatraz, this was not.

The Sunday of my first week was approaching and I went to the MP desk in the guardhouse.

"Excuse me, Corporal, but am I allowed to attend church?"

The MP eyed me very coolly, looking to see if I was joking, or trying to get a rise out of him.

"I can assure you that I usually attend church on base," I added, giving some credence to my request.

Out came the huge book of RAF regulations and the corporal proceeded to flip through it.

"Actually, yes, you can, with a police escort."

"Thanks, put me down for Sunday please."

When my two friends heard about this, they too applied for church and despite the fact that the MP's knew that it would probably be their first visit ever, they had to grant the request.

Sunday came and off we went to church, accompanied by a police escort. We had a special pew at the front of the church, and so down the aisle came one MP leading the three of us prisoners with another MP bringing up the rear. To the congregation we must have looked like a same sex wedding procession with a military theme.

Needless to say, my cell mates did not accompany me on the following Sunday, and a few days later they went to another base for their court martial. Despite my enquiries I never did find out what happened to them. As for Corporal McCormick, I had contact with him on my return, but the incident was never mentioned again. He finished his National Service long before I did and returned to civilian life, as I did later on.

I served a few days more and then went back to my squadron. As an "ex-con," I had a certain celebrity status. However, this didn't last very long.

HOPPY   RON   JOCH   DAVE   DEREK.

REG   VERNON   JOHN   ANDY.

**Derek (2nd from the back row, on right) with No. 17 RAF Regiment,
Celle, Germany, 1954**

ENTER LAUGHING

As a young man growing up in Liverpool, England, one of my favorite things was listening to comedy shows on the radio. Some shows were what are now called situation comedies, and others were stand-up comedy acts. And then there was one in particular which was the forerunner to Monty Python's Flying Circus with its absurd, surreal humor called "The Goon Show," featuring Peter Sellers who led all the craziness.

When the show was over, I would meet with my friends, who all shared my enthusiasm for these comedy programs. We would discuss the best lines and act out the situations, laughing at it all over again.

For my friends this was enough, but I wanted to take it further. I admired the clever writing, absurd situations and the structure of the comedy. What's more, I felt that I could do the same, if not better.

Seeing the humor and absurdity in life was an important part of who I was. If these two companions were not immediately apparent, I would seek them out.

In school I was viewed with a wary eye by the teachers. since my questions, although hopefully intelligent enough, were often laced with mischief. I found that humor was both a weapon and a suit of armor, to be used accordingly. Arrogance and pomposity were such fun targets that I could laugh at any bullies around me without them even knowing it. I also found, as I grew older, that humor could be seductive. The fact that I was hardly the best looking guy in the gang seemed to make little difference if making the girls laugh gave me an advantage.

All of this led to my thinking of comedy writing as a career. I began writing to the top comedians and writers, mainly at the BBC, for information and guidance. The replies were sometimes helpful, but in effect said "If you want to write comedy, write comedy."

I then set my sights on a radio comedian called Ken Platt. I chose him because he was a working man's comedian and his humor was something I could relate to. He appeared not only on BBC variety shows but at factories around the country on a very popular show called "Workers Playtime." Without contacting him first, I sent him jokes that I felt he could use. For a while I did not receive a reply.

A few weeks later I was lying in a hospital ward recovering from a soccer injury and listening to the radio through headphones. It was a live edition of "Workers Playtime" and comedian Ken Platt was introduced. He began his storytelling and then I began to hear jokes that I had written for him.

I took off my headphones and began shouting to people in the beds around me:

"Tune in to Workers Playtime, it's Ken Platt and those are my jokes!"

But how did I know that those were my jokes? How could I prove that these were the jokes I had written and sent to him? But I did know. They were practically word for word as I had written them.

I immediately wrote a letter to Mr. Platt telling him that I had heard his show and was delighted that he had been able to use my material and that perhaps we could come to some arrangement.

He replied and suggested that I visit him at his home which was a short train ride from where I lived. On the journey to the meeting, I reflected on how surreal it was that this 24-year-old Liverpool lad was about to discuss a business arrangement with a well-known entertainer. Naturally, I was extremely nervous. I tried to marshal my thoughts but without much success.

It was a rather strange meeting, and he was a rather strange man. His comedic persona was that of a bluff, hearty, working-class man with a very cheerful take on life. But what I saw in person was an anxious, very shy fellow who could hardly put two words together. Luckily, he had his agent with him. One of the more bizarre aspects of the meeting was the fact that Ken Platt's mother, who lived with him, would shout from another room and he would leave immediately to go to her.

I reflected that this was nothing at all like the glamorous Hollywood show biz meetings I saw in the movies.

Actually, this worked for me. When I arrived I was a nervous wreck and had no idea what I was getting into. What would I say? What did I want? But now I began to relax. They didn't know either.

His agent took over.

"The BBC wants Ken to move from radio to television and are pressing him to come up with his own tv situation comedy series, so obviously he will need more writers. Perhaps you could you submit some ideas and we can take it from there."

We talked about his stand-up act but with no mention of payment for my jokes that he had used. Then, as the meeting was coming to an end, the agent said, "Let me look at the material you have already given Ken for his stand-up and I will be in touch." I am convinced that if he had not mentioned it, I certainly wouldn't have. Something told me that I was not cut out for negotiating show business contracts.

A short while later I received a letter from Ken Platt's office with a money order. I was not even given the dignity of a check. It was not a large amount of money, but I had no idea of what I was entitled to anyway. Of course, I knew that comedians are notorious for avoiding payment for material and for stealing jokes wherever they can.

I still sent scripts and ideas to Platt and to various people in the business without much success, and then I became caught up with my insurance career, exams, marriage and eventually emigration to the U.S. Ken Platt never did move from radio to television.

When I arrived in New York I attended some comedy workshops in hopes of rekindling my non-existent comedy writing career. However, that did not happen. Life took over in the form of finding a job and settling down in my new country.

Over time I found some minor compensation in the fact that as a business executive I was frequently invited to make speeches. These speeches were an opportunity to craft mini stand-up acts, warming up the audience before the actual speech.

Still, it was hardly the comedy career I had hoped for.

INVITATION TO THE DANCE

"Going to the dance," as it was called, was a sort of mating ritual engaged in by most young people in Liverpool in the fifties, and at the age of seventeen I joined in and began to frequent dance halls with my friends.

There were ballroom dances going on most days of the week but the local dance on Saturday night was by far the most important. Friday was pay day at the local factories and that meant giving a portion of your wages to the household for room and board. Since everyone lived at home, we then would have enough in our pockets for a fun weekend of drinking and dancing.

Throughout Saturday afternoon there was a palpable excitement in the air leading up to the big night ahead. We would see the young girls with their hair in large, rather ugly curlers keeping their "wash and set" in place for the evening. But being seen around town with such an unglamorous appearance never seemed to embarrass the girls at all. It was as though they knew that their full flowering, to be witnessed later on, would more than make up for this temporary lapse.

Saturday afternoons also meant congregating at the local record store to buy the latest hits from America. Not only did we buy the Johnny Ray, Frankie Laine, and Guy Mitchell records but we sang them continuously until we knew all the words by heart. Those songs of love, longing, and heartbreak gave expression to what surely many of us were feeling at that time. They also helped to transport us from our rather confining existence in that working-class town to the land of promise and glamour—America.

When the doors of the dancehall opened, the girls trooped in for a much-anticipated evening of dancing. However, for the first two hours they simply danced with one another since the boys were usually gathered at one of the local pubs, fueling up on liquid courage that would help them later on when it was time to approach a girl and ask her to dance.

A certain amount of pent-up energy found its outlet in violence, which often spilled over at local dances. There were certain dance halls that acquired a reputation for fighting. The drinking had a great deal to do with it, but it was also part of the culture. Liverpool has long had a reputation for humor and many of England's famous comedians were born there. But beneath the wit and humor so often associated with Liverpudlians, there was also a darker side—a hard edge that was well-honed after years of poverty and deprivation, giving its people a sense of resentment against the rest of the world. It was an "us" versus "them" mentality, justified or not, and this is what took hold on those Saturday nights. A wrong word or simply dancing with the wrong girl could easily lead to a fistfight. Luckily, it was only that—it was unusual for weapons to be used.

One of the male rites of passage at that time meant looking mature enough to obtain a pint at the tender age of seventeen, since the legal drinking age at that time was eighteen. Actually, since drinking was so much a part of the Liverpool culture it was very rare that anyone was turned down. But it did happen on occasion, and when it did, it was quite the humiliation. The unlucky fellow would then have to slink out the door in search of better luck at the next pub while his friends chortled into their beers.

At 10 o'clock the pubs stopped serving and it was time to saunter down to the dance hall for the next part of the evening. As we flung open the doors to the dance hall we were immediately met with a feast for the senses—vibrant melodies from the live band echoing throughout the hall, a sea of dancers spinning and swaying on the main floor, and the lively chatter of teenagers buzzing with excitement and anticipation.

But behind the strutting and noisy bravado of the boys and the prattling and preening of the girls, there was somehow a sense of shyness and awkwardness of youth not full formed and knowing it.

We would then circle the floor searching for girls we knew and with whom we felt comfortable asking to dance. And who knows, perhaps later when our courage was really up, we could venture further afield and ask a stranger. It was at one such dance hall on a Saturday night that I did just that, and met the woman who would be my wife for the next 40 years.

I scanned the dance floor and spotted a petite blonde girl talking to her friends. They stood on the edge of the dance floor, obviously hoping to be asked to dance but of course would never admit it.

I approached the blonde to ask for a dance and off we went. The first dance, a waltz, went smoothly, as did our conversation—it was all very sedate and polite.

I soon learned that she had attended a top girl's school in Liverpool on a scholarship. We immediately had something in common, as I too had attended a prestigious school, the Liverpool Institute, on scholarship. She told me that she lived a few hundred yards from the dance hall. That seemed like a minor detail at the time, but it loomed large as I would later come to realize. Oh, and her name was Marion.

By this time the band had moved on from the mild, dignified waltz and foxtrot to the more upbeat jive, and then it was onto my favorites, the Latin American rumba and sambas.

I again asked Marion for a dance which happened to be a rumba. I must admit that I may have gone a little overboard with these more exotic dances.

Fueled by a couple of pints during the dance intermission, I threw in some extra twirling and flashy side stepping for good measure.

After our dance I walked Marion back to her friends, and then she turned to me and said "You think you're hot stuff, don't you?" To which I immediately replied, "Yes, I do rather..." She tried not to smile but was not very successful.

At the end of night came the ultimate test of striking up the nerve to ask a girl if you could take her home. But it was all rather innocent and simple then. For instance, there was no question of staying the night since everyone lived at home with parents who allowed very little freedom, especially to girls. Although the neighborhood was poor, people had their family pride. Every family wanted to avoid the terrible humiliation of having a daughter "get into trouble" which was a euphemism for getting pregnant. However, we were seventeen and eighteen years old, so our hormones were bouncing off the walls. But because of the social mores of the day, they would have to settle down and wait for a more appropriate time.

It was the last dance of the night, and I again sought Marion out for a dance. I then asked if I could walk her home. She mentioned again that she lived just down the street, very close to the dance hall, so it was hardly worth it. I told Marion I would like to walk her home anyway, and she finally relented. She had another plan in mind, an escape plan to be exact, and she would put it into effect anytime a young man would offer to walk her home.

This "exit strategy," as I would come to find out later, was her way of avoiding being walked home, and all the awkwardness that could potentially go along with it. If a young man was waiting to walk her home at the end of the night, Marion did her best to slip out unnoticed—she would bid her friends goodnight, quickly grab her coat, and head right for the exit doors. Marion would even go as far as to hide out in the ladies room, praying that her unsuspecting suitor waiting in the lobby would eventually give up in frustration and leave. When she felt like the coast was clear, she would then hightail it out of there, hurrying down the street to the safety of her house.

In keeping with her elaborate escape plan, Marion let me know that she might be a while saying goodbye to her friends. But I simply told her I would be waiting for her outside when the dance was over.

But unknowingly I had decided to go outside

a little early, foiling her plan. Marion soon found herself bursting through the doors of the dance hall, rushing down the steps, and right into my arms.

Naturally, I made a joke out of it, saying something to the effect of, "My, you are in a hurry to see me!" Being caught in mid-getaway, she could not have been any more flustered, or mortified. Needless to say, she did not appreciate my comment at the time.

So that night Marion let me walk her home.

Under the watchful eye of her father who was waiting on the doorstep, I bid Marion a hasty goodnight, with a promise to be in touch. Somehow I knew I would be....

THE WEDDING

A popular Victorian music hall song called "Daisy" has a line it: "It won't be a stylish marriage, I can't afford a carriage..."

That just about sums up my wedding day. But this was Liverpool in the 1950's and what exactly did I expect? Liverpool working-class weddings have many endearing qualities: love, warmth, sincerity, and lots of laughter, but no one could accuse them

Marion and Derek, St. Michael's Church, Garston, 1957

of having style. For one thing, people simply could not afford real comfort and elegance and, even if they tried, they would be accused of "getting above themselves."

Marion and I had known each other two years, which was not a long time in those days when people courted for years as they saved money for a home of their own. But we were very much in love, and the idea of waiting for a few years to be married was excruciating. We could not bear to be away from each other for any length of time and even travelled to and from work together even though we would be seeing each other that evening. We wrote letters to each other every day with my brothers and sisters acting as letter carriers and go-betweens. It led to a great deal of teasing in my large family in which it was almost impossible to keep a secret. However, romance in Liverpool in those days was in short supply and I suspect that my family rather enjoyed having star-crossed lovers literally in their own backyard.

In 1957, we became engaged and set the wedding date for June 10th, which was Whitsuntide Monday, a national holiday in England. I had been saving money to take a vacation in Spain with my mates, but I decided to spend the money on an engagement ring for Marion who thought this romantic and gallant of me. Not so my friends, who thought I was crazy to choose marriage over sun, sand, sex, and Sangria (and in Spain)!!

Hastily arranged marriages at that time usually meant one thing—the bride was pregnant and I am sure that the thought crossed the minds of our respective families. They also raised their doubts about our relative youth (Marion was nineteen, I was twenty-two), our lack of money, no established career, etc. Indeed, this was all true but we went ahead anyway.

The day was upon us and the wedding party began to arrive at St. Michael's, the local church we had been attending for many years. Most of the guests came by bus, with wedding cars only for the bride and her stepfather.

For an occasion like this, a number of neighbors would turn up to watch or even sit at the back of the church. Occasions like weddings and funerals were events to be savored in an otherwise drab existence.

After the ceremony as Marion and I walked back up the aisle wearing smiles that would last the next forty years, we were jolted by the appearance of a figure who jumped out of the last pew. We stopped suddenly, and I could see that Marion was visibly shaken. As I turned to her, the man left as quickly as he appeared.

Marion composed herself and told me that the man was her real father whom she had not seen for a number of years. I already knew that he had left the family when she was a little girl although I had never met him. We both concluded that the poor man merely wanted to see his daughter on her wedding day, although we also agreed that he might have done so in a less dramatic fashion.

Then it was on to the reception which was rather a grand name for the fairly modest occasion. Marion's stepfather had owned a grocery store which was now empty, and he had insisted that after the painting and wallpapering it would be just the room for the wedding breakfast. In that dingy corner shop with the smell of fresh paint lingering in the air, we sat down to sandwiches, cake, and tea. We toasted with sherry since champagne was something we only saw in the movies.

This rather meager celebration did not bother Marion or me since we were just counting the hours until we were on the train heading for our honeymoon and new life together.

After the meal everybody was off to the pub to meet up with other friends who wanted to celebrate with us. We all enjoyed a lively time replete with pints and happy toasts. Then it was back to the shop for a good old-fashioned "knees-up," which was drinking, singing, dancing, and party pieces thrown in for good measure.

Everyone was having a wonderful time, and the party was in full swing. But soon Marion and I had to leave for the train station, and even we felt a twinge at leaving such a happy group.

We waited for what seemed like an eternity for our taxi driver until I realized that he was the person everyone was cheering as he vigorously danced a solo at our party, sweating profusely and drinking from a very large beer glass at frequent intervals. We dragged him away and reached the station in one piece which was surprising considering the fact that he insisted on turning around to us in the back seat several times to congratulate us.

There was one final note of minor drama to end our day. The beer I had quaffed had taken its toll and I desperately had to find a men's room even though the train was due to leave at any minute. I did, much to my new bride's dismay. As I ran out of the rest room the train was indeed just moving out of the station and I managed to climb aboard to find Marion a nervous wreck.

She was fond of telling people that the incident was a clear omen that during our life together there would never be a dull moment.

As usual, she was oh so right....

PART 3

MY NOT SO BRILLIANT
CAREER

O ur van came to a halt at the end of the street.
"Ok, lads!" said our sales supervisor. "Time to sell
some cleaners. Let's go!"

Along with my three fellow salesmen, I jumped out
and grabbed the brown boxes that contained our product,
a German manufactured vacuum cleaner made by a
company called National. We were to fan out through the
neighborhood and begin knocking on doors. Hopefully
gaining entry to the home, we could then perform a
demonstration and "Voila!" the vacuum was sold.

Ah, if it were only that easy. All too often the door
did not open, of course. It could be that people were out,
but sometimes the people were home, knew the game,
and simply did not want to open the door. Sometimes a
curtain would move slightly, and the person inside would
slyly peek out. On occasion, just for the hell of it, I would
put my face to the window and smilingly point to the door,
almost shaming the householder to open it. Welcome to
the career, if that is the right word, of door-to-door selling.

When a door opened our opening gambit was the following:

"Good day, Madam!" (This was almost without
exception, a woman's world, being Britain in the 1950's.)

"My company is in the area demonstrating a brand
new cleaning product (never say vacuum cleaner) that we

bring you straight from The Ideal Homes Exhibition in London."

This was not entirely true. Yes, it was a new product. However, we had no connection at all with the Ideal Homes Exhibition which displayed the latest in household appliances and was a name instantly recognized by every housewife in Britain.

The other deception in the statement was that we were there not to just demonstrate, but to sell. This was something we could never admit, otherwise we would never make it over the threshold. Those salesmen with a conscience, and I counted myself among them, had to preserve whatever shred of integrity we had by convincing ourselves that we were selling a fine product that the consumer needed, which would serve them well for years to come. The irony was not lost on us that despite its excellence the product was German, something that only a few years after World War II it would hardly be appropriate to mention.

The neighborhood we were selling to was poor and working-class, located in a small mining district outside of Liverpool. The houses, all government subsidized, stood attached to one another. Each had a tiny patch of grass in front, and more often than not, it was neglected and overgrown. Whoever wrote "I Left My Heart in An English Garden" did not have this greenery in mind.

Getting people in this area to spend money on an expensive vacuum cleaner was going to be a real challenge indeed.

What on earth was I doing here anyway?

My family was appalled when I left my steady, respectable job at the Westminster Bank to become a salesman. The fact is, I had to leave the job for financial reasons. My wife Marion was pregnant and would soon be leaving her job and we simply could not make it on just my steady and respectable, but measly, bank pay. Luckily, I had my wife's encouragement. She felt that if it did not work out, I was young and could try something else.

I had answered an advertisement for a salesman that promised a salary three times more than what I was earning at the bank. Of course, one first had to sell the product, but I felt confident I could do the job at the highest level. My interview was perfunctory to say the least. This should have told me something, plus the fact that the door-to-door aspect of the sales job was withheld to almost the end of the interview. After a three-day sales course (another clue, perhaps?) I was thrown into the breach. It was commission only, but with a base amount to see one through a dry period—a very short dry period. Otherwise, you were out.

I was now part of the sales team. My fellow salesmen, although not exactly misfits, had not had very successful careers to date. One had been fired from his job as a wages clerk, another arrived from a different city after a messy divorce, and the other was starting a door-to-door business and was looking for some pointers (a little late for that, I thought but..). The beauty of this kind of sales career was the "no experience necessary" aspect, trumpeted in every advertisement for salesmen.

Once inside a house it was almost an unwritten rule that one would never be turfed out. These were very kind, hospitable people. A cup of tea was always offered and must never be refused. By accepting tea, one became a guest rather than a salesman.

I would usually be in a very small living room, with a couch, two armchairs and a coal fire burning in the small fireplace. Sometimes there was a television set, a new technology in those days, and always a good sign that the family would be willing to buy appliances.

The carpet was never wall to wall and was usually just a piece covering part of the room. If they had no vacuum cleaner, I could count on the carpet being filthy. This was mining country with lots of coal dust to go around. There was a coal burning fire to add to the dust problem. Amazing to think that many homes at that time did not have a vacuum cleaner. They managed with a brush or a sweeper.

My first demonstration was something of a disaster. I unpacked the cleaner and began to assemble the hose to it, trying to look as though I knew what I was doing and disguise the fact that I was new to the job. When I pressed the "Start" button (at least I got that right), clouds of dust swirled up from the carpet and filled the room. In my nervousness I had attached the blowing end of the cleaner instead of the suction connection. When the dust settled, I managed to make out the lady of the house with her two children sitting on the couch looking like three raccoons with black dust around their eyes. Goodness knows what I looked like.

It was a measure of the kind of people they were in those poor neighborhoods that they did not get angry at what happened—they were only concerned for me and my embarrassment. "Don't worry, love, we all make mistakes" and "It's very powerful, isn't it?" However, I don't recall that they actually bought my vacuum cleaner.

There were one or two other mishaps along the way. I blew a fuse in one house when I plugged into the electrical circuit, causing a temporary power outage. In another house I nearly decapitated a dear old lady when I was showing her how she could clean the stair carpet. As I began to demonstrate, the cleaner came right off the hose and slid down the stairs at breakneck speed as she was following me up.

But inevitably I began to get the hang of it, with more demonstrations leading to sales. After several rejections in a row there was always the temptation to quit for a while, go for a coffee with other salesmen, moan about how bad the neighborhood was, grumble about why we should have gone elsewhere, and always lamenting the one that got away. However, I knew that staying with it and continually knocking on doors would eventually win the day. But for how long? There was the rub...

To sell two cleaners in a week would get a decent wage, and to sell three would give me far more than I earned in the bank. But selling three cleaners a week was a soul-destroying undertaking. The sales force changed constantly, and after a while I was the veteran in the group. New people came in like so much cannon fodder.

I eventually realized that this was not a life's career, but rather an interesting stop along the way and just one part of my life's experience. I decided to quit after having been there a year, which was much longer than most.

Sadly, another factor figured in my decision, which was that Marion lost the baby at birth. Eventually, she wanted to go back to work, and our financial situation would work itself out.

I soon began another career which was to last over 35 years.

GINGER—PART 2

In the mid-1950's, my friends and I were all demobilized from our two-year National Service at around the same time. All except Ginger, who had volunteered for three years in the Royal Navy for the extra pay. We would see him on his furloughs home, and he would regale us with tales of life onboard the ship. Many of these revolved around the tradition that went back to the time of Lord Nelson, whereby a tot of rum was given twice a day to all sailors.

Ginger was convinced that most of the crew were in a permanent state of inebriation, including himself. This went a long way in explaining his behavior when he left the service.

The guys still hung out together but not as often. By this time, a few of us had serious girlfriends so the lads settled on getting together on Friday nights as our night out. We usually went to the pub for a few pints but if there was a new movie playing in downtown Liverpool, we would catch a showing there.

One day, the gang and I were waiting in a very long line at the cinema for the next performance. It was Ginger, Dava Jones, Bobby Whiteside, Frankie Yeadon, Ray and Les Hill aka "The Pilly's," and myself. As we were chatting together, an elderly couple in rather faded old clothes stood near us, not in line but away from the queue. Suddenly, they each whipped out a violin from under their coats and began frenetically playing a piece of classical music. They were "buskers"-street performers who played for the crowd lining up for the movies or theatre which was a common sight in those days.

However, the incongruity of this shabby old couple suddenly plunging into the music so quickly and dramatically tickled Ginger no end. When he thought something was very funny, he reacted physically. He would draw in his breath and the laughter would start bubbling up inside him. He would slowly sink to his knees like a boxer going down for the count, then would stagger around, reaching for something or someone to hold on to. Then the laughter would come pouring out, enveloping those around him who couldn't help joining in, although sometimes not being entirely sure just what the joke was.

That was Ginger at his best, finding the very heart of humor in the most unlikely places. My friends and I would find ourselves going from serious to hilarious in a matter of seconds at his prompting.

I remember watching a movie starring J. Carroll Naish, an actor who played many gangster roles in the "B" movies from the 1940's. There was a scene in which Naish, a gang boss, was berating his men who were cowering around him. He then took his coat off to hang on a chair and suddenly Ginger went into one of his paroxysms of laughter. "Look at his pants!" he gasped. Sure enough this tough gangster had a pair of pants on almost to his shoulders and held up by tiny suspenders. He looked like a circus clown and when it was pointed out we too were screaming with laughter. This was yet another example of Ginger inhabiting his own "Theatre of the Absurd."

But soon we would see Ginger less and less as time went by. He had left the Navy, but the Navy had not left him. He was drinking as though he was constantly trying to keep up with his daily rum ration.

Like all working-class lads of that time, we were beer drinkers. Two or three pints would see us through the evening and give us that "buzz" that we called "merry." Drinking "shorts" which meant whiskey, gin, or rum, was usually reserved for Christmas, birthdays and holidays. And so when Ginger ordered a short, it drew attention.

"I didn't know it was your birthday, Ginger, are you buying for everyone?"

Ginger, defensively, would say "This beer is weak. I needed a pick me up."

And so a pattern began. More and more he was chasing his pint with whiskey or rum. It started to affect his behavior. Rather than join in the banter, after a couple of rounds he would sit there just looking into the distance.

I approached him on it.

"You know Ginger, we go out together to have fun and not to drink for the sake of drinking. You are an important part of the laughs and I hate to see you so out of it. It makes me wonder what the hell is going on."

"I enjoy a short. I'll be fine," he would say.

But he wasn't fine, and there were other things happening in our lives that complicated the situation even more.

Marion liked him a lot, and really enjoyed his humor. She encouraged him to join us in going to the dance or to the movies. She even introduced him to her girlfriends, and we did double date. But Ginger showed no real interest in any of them.

For some time Marion and I had given some thought to emigrating to the US, and eventually made our decision to leave. We continued socializing with our friends and with Ginger, but it wasn't the same. He was subdued, although not drinking too much either (in public anyway) but I sensed through conversations with his father that he drank heavily at home.

His father was a very kind, quiet man and had a wonderful relationship with Ginger. They had been together ever since the mother died and there was a real affection between them. When Ginger first joined our group, his father was very happy. They lived in an area near the docks that was a breeding ground for petty criminals and violent activity, and he might well have ended up in the wrong group. But now he too was concerned with "Billy's" drinking (Mr. Martin never called him Ginger).

Marion and I left Liverpool that November. Ginger was among those at the party the night before and was with the crowd on the Liverpool dock to wave us goodbye.

When in New York I wrote to Ginger often, telling him about life in America, but he rarely replied. I would hear scraps of news about Ginger from other friends. He seemed to cut himself off from them and he was still drinking.

One day a few years later I received a phone call from my brother in Liverpool telling me that there had been a fire at Ginger's house where he now lived alone, and he had died. Apparently, he had been drinking and had fallen into the fire.

I still think of him often, especially when I am savoring something absurd and ridiculous, feeling quite certain that he would have felt the same way too.

EMIGRANT FEVER

Marion was extremely bright and excelled academically. She was consistently at the top of her class at her prestigious girls high school and her teachers had implored her to apply to university. However, despite the fact that government grants would pay for her continuing education, her mother would have none of it, and insisted on her leaving school and taking a job as a secretary. Marion defended her mother's action by pointing out that she had raised Marion and her brother as a single parent with little money, and should not be blamed for wanting financial help if Marion could provide it. Nevertheless, there was a quiet resentment on Marion's part at not being allowed to take advantage of the opportunity for higher education.

Her mother was a moody, difficult woman and Marion's relationship with her was not an easy one. This made leaving her, if the opportunity should arise, easier than it might have been otherwise.

Marion and I were now enjoying interests which set us apart from our friends and family. She had taken a position as secretary to the General Manager of the Workers Education Association, an organization funded by the trades union in the UK. The WEA arranged courses in literature, theatre, film, and art for its members. These often took place on weekends at stately houses around Great Britain with lectures by academics from the best universities. Marion often had to go on these weekends as an organizer and in order to be with her I went along too and joined the classes. She often sat in on courses when her work was done. We soon found ourselves immersed in the "Angry Young Man" writings of John Osborne, Arnold Wesker, and Alan Sillitoe who were saying many of the same things about class in England that I had been voicing to the deaf ears of friends, family, and anyone else who would listen.

Then it was on to American literature and the plays of Arthur Miller, Tennessee Williams, and other writers to whose work we had access. We loved it all and could not believe that we had stumbled on to this treasure trove of learning. We tried to persuade friends to join us on these weekends or night classes but had little success. This eagerness for learning was viewed with some suspicion. This was not something that people of our class did. It was better to know one's place, and not try to emulate one's elders and "betters."

I was still with the bank at this time and Marion and I would joke about my prospects, since promotions for young men like me moved at a glacial pace.

I would say "If I keep my nose to the grindstone, finish all of my exams and don't kill anyone in the office, with a bit of luck I could be a bank manager by the time I'm 50!"

"Yes," said Marion, "and we could have a little semi-detached in the suburbs with our two dear ones, Penelope and little Jeremy who could play in the tiny back garden. Isn't life wonderful??"

I began exploring bank positions in British colonies overseas: Rhodesia, West Africa, Australia and India. I had heard that these banks wanted young Brits to staff their offices.

They did indeed. "You are just the type of fellow we are looking for. Young, well-trained, and working on your exams. We would love to meet you" was the type of response I usually received.

I did have a couple of interviews but soon learned that there was a problem. At that time, Marion and I were planning to be married and, if we went overseas, it would be as a married couple. However, I was twenty-two and the overseas banks had a minimum age of twenty-six for married men, at which point the salary scale was adequate and not before. They suggested that I join the bank overseas and have Marion join me in 4 years. My answer to that was easy. I bid farewell to my imperialist banking career.

Then, during all of this soul-searching, enter my cousin Nancy, on a visit to Liverpool from her home in Brooklyn, New York to see family. We saw a lot of Nancy on this visit and began to talk about life in America. I had always had a great interest in the USA but in the 1950's it was some far away country only accessible by movies, books and theatre. I was hungry for everything I could learn about America and spent hours with

Cousin Nancy with Derek, 1961

Nancy talking about her life there. Before she left for home, she said that if we ever did decide to emigrate, she would sponsor us.

These were the cross currents that were leading Marion and me away from Britain—our general dissatisfaction with the life we saw ahead of us, Marion's difficult relationship with her mother, and our conviction that there were opportunities elsewhere that would give us a much different life to the one laid out for us in England.

At first, no one around us took us seriously. In the 1950's people were emigrating to Australia and New Zealand in large numbers, but those countries were British, after all. Nobody set off to go live in America. The quota system for the British going to America was never close to being filled.

To the British, America at that time was the movies and every American was either a cowboy or a gangster. It was all very entertaining, but to the British in general, especially my friends, it might as well have been on another planet.

There were also the practical objections from our families. We would be arriving with no job, no home and no health insurance safety net so beloved by the British, especially the working people. Marion and I forged ahead with our plans and soon we had not only our papers with Nancy's sponsorship, but a guarantee of a job for Marion at Nancy's company, Remington Rand. I received letters inviting me to interview with various insurance companies when I arrived in New York.

When everyone realized that we were determined to emigrate they wished us well. "I wish I had your courage. I'd love to leave this bloody place, there's nothing much for us here." These comments were always accompanied by the inevitable excuses such as "I'm too old," "I couldn't leave my mother," "I'd never find a job," etc. We didn't care. The die was cast. Our adventure would begin very soon.

WELCOME TO AMERICA

It was a cold November day in 1961, and the Cunard liner R.M.S. Sylvania eased its way towards the mouth of New York harbor, with the Statue of Liberty only a short distance away.

My wife Marion and I joined the crowd of other passengers on deck waiting excitedly to pass under the famous statue as thousands of immigrants had done before us. Then, as I was savoring the moment, reality set in.

"Derek, you're shivering, it's freezing out here. You will catch your death of cold. That's the last thing we need right now. Put a coat or a sweater on. You have time."

Marion was right of course. Playing fast and loose with my health at this point was, well, suicidal. I could still hear my older brothers urging me to rethink our plans to emigrate to the USA.

"You know there's no National Health scheme in America, right? They let people die on the street if they have no insurance."

"Yes, I know, and I promise to do my best to keep us both alive," I would reply.

"Don't be funny, we're only trying to help." This was an unusually sharp reprimand from my eldest brother, Bill.

"Sorry, but we will be fine," I said, more in hope than knowledge.

With that conversation ringing in my ears, I dove down the stairs to our cabin, grabbed a thick sweater and charged back to Marion's side just as we were approaching Lady Liberty. It was such a dramatic moment, and everyone was in such awe, so I refrained from commenting on how the statue's greenish color made her look just a little moldy.

As we continued on towards the pier, I saw all of the cars lined up on the quay and I was fascinated by the length of the vehicles. The tail fins of the Cadillacs, Buicks, and Oldsmobiles protruded out into the water, and I naturally compared them to the small box-like like cars I had known in England. That was the beginning of the inevitable comparisons with my old country that would continue for some time, giving those early days in New York a surreal quality.

We were being met by my cousin Nancy who, as an American citizen, had sponsored our emigration to the USA.

Nancy was a "G.I. bride" having married an American serviceman in England and joining him in the U.S. at the age of 19. The marriage did not last, but they had a son, Barry, with whom she now lived in Bensonhurst, Brooklyn, along with her new husband, Jerry Zaccaria.

When we did not see Nancy right away, I gave in to a mild panic and I left Marion with the luggage to go look around. But I need not have worried. When I returned, Nancy and Marion were locked in an embrace of hugs and tears in which I soon joined. Jerry had gone for the car, and we were ready for our first American adventure which was the ride from the city to Brooklyn.

When Jerry came with the car it was an old Buick, which was a far cry from the sleek, glamorous vehicles

I had seen on the pier. It had a large hole in the floor, and had I played the Englishman, I would have politely pretended not to notice. However, I didn't, and I asked if Jerry intended to put his feet through the hole and pedal us back to Brooklyn. Had I "Americanized" so quickly? Nevertheless, Jerry thought it funny, so I suppose we were off to a great start.

Jerry Zaccaria was one of three brothers. His twin, Albert, worked in a funeral parlor, and Jerry held some vague position with the Transit Authority in New York. Both jobs were courtesy of the eldest brother Paul, who was a leading member of the Gambino Mafia family. Yes, you heard correctly. I won't say it again.

I shall never forget the frantic phone call I received from Nancy a few months after we had arrived in New York.

"Derek, I know you read Time magazine. Do you have the copy out today?"

I did indeed. She gave me the number of the page to turn to. It was an elaborate table of organization of the five Mafia families in the USA. Near the top of the Gambino chart was the name Paul Zaccaria, Jerry's brother. I cut Nancy off in mid-apology about this association. Jerry, to Marion and me, had been nothing but warm and welcoming since we had arrived. Nobody needed to apologize to me about him or his family. It was Bensonhurst, Brooklyn in 1961, and Jerry's brother's connection to the mob was what it was.

Jerry was a very likable man who welcomed Marion and myself as though we were his own. After discovering that I had a love of sports, he enjoyed telling me about the American games of football, baseball, and basketball. He also had a love for sports but with a different slant.

Jerry was a problem gambler and was constantly betting on the games, though our time at their apartment was so short that we did not see evidence of this. To us, Jerry was charming and warm, however I did learn later of phones being ripped out of the wall and furniture being broken when a bad result came in.

Nancy and Jerry's apartment was a fifth floor walk-up in a middle class Jewish / Italian section of Brooklyn. It had two bedrooms, a dining room and a kitchen. For the three of them it was more than adequate. However, with Marion and I sleeping on a pull-out bed and taking over the living room, it was obvious, despite Nancy's protestations, that this would be a very temporary stay indeed.

Jerry, Nancy, Marion, and Derek, Bensonhurst, Brooklyn, December 1961

In the meantime, everywhere we turned it was all so new to us—the tv programs, the supermarket, the food (what on earth is a bagel??), and of course the people. Nancy took us downstairs and outside the apartment building to introduce us to the group of mainly older Jewish women from the building who gathered there most days and sat around to chat. All of them were very friendly, but much more direct than a similar group of British ladies would be.

Nancy's mother and mine had been very close sisters and the two families had been equally close, living in the same neighborhood. She had a good position in the Personnel Department of Remington Rand which would prove to be very helpful in getting Marion a job. She was warm, lively, and kind, and determined to give us the best possible start in our new home.

On the first Saturday night of our arrival, I remember staying up late talking with Nancy and Jerry. At around midnight Jerry suggested to Marion and me that we take a walk over to Kings Highway, the main thoroughfare nearby, to pick up the Sunday papers. It seemed a strange time to be going out for the paper but after only a relatively few hours in America we were beginning to be surprised by less and less.

The crowds and hustle and bustle on Kings Highway were busier than Liverpool at midday. Stores and restaurants were open, and people were everywhere. When Jerry handed me the New York Times I almost buckled under the weight of the paper. I couldn't wait to get home to read it from cover to cover.

On the first Sunday morning Jerry asked if I would like to go down to his club. This was where he would meet his friends and presumably receive money for his bets from the day before, or more likely pay his debts. Hungry for all the new experiences I could get, I agreed.

"Grab your hat and coat, it's cold," said Jerry.

We drove the short distance and pulled up at a store front. Jerry jumped out of the car very quickly and ran into the club, leaving me to follow. I trailed in behind him and could hear him shouting his hello's and people shouting back, "Hey, Mummy!" (That was his street name.) How's it going?"

I then walked in the door and for a split second there was a frozen silence as everyone stopped and looked at me. Then there was a scraping of chairs with one or two chairs turned over as people jumped to their feet. I didn't realize it then, but some of these men were mob guys. They were small time perhaps, but nevertheless the sight of my coming in the door with a fedora and raincoat, looking like Elliot Ness was a little unnerving to say the least. Then Jerry stepped in. He had a sly smile on his face which indicated he had planned the whole thing—running ahead to allow me to come in alone. Jerry calmed everyone down and told them who I was, telling them that I was family and a new immigrant. Then I was mobbed (sorry about that).

"Hey, have some anisette!"

"Welcome to America!"

"How you like America, eh?"

It was yet another wonderful welcome. I had been in America less than two days.

Going Away Party, 1961

Cunard R.M.S. Sylvania

Cunard R.M.S. Sylvania

SOCCER AMERICAN STYLE

From the time that I was old enough to play in the street outside of our house in Liverpool, I have loved playing football, or soccer as it is called in America, although that term still grates on me. The people of Liverpool have such a passion for the sport that it's almost a religion.

First, I played street football and was on school teams, then it was neighborhood leagues right up to the time I was ready to leave for a new life in America at age 26.

My wife Marion and I were packing for our voyage to New York.

"Do you think it is the height of optimism to pack my football boots?" I asked Marion.

"I'd say that the height of optimism is leaving England to live in America, without either of us having a job. It would be hard to top that," she said.

Point taken—into the suitcase the boots were tossed.

Upon arrival in New York, our first priority was to get a job, which we both did rather quickly. Marion was working at Remington Rand as a secretary within ten days of our arrival in New York.

I was still in the middle of interviews when Marion came home one day to say that she was chatting with a bank guard, a Scotsman, who was a soccer referee. As he described it, there was a thriving, vibrant soccer scene in the New York area. He said that if I was interested in a trial with the semi-professional team, the New York Italians, I should contact him.

I did just that, and soon I was over on Randall's Island to try my luck in the new world of American soccer. I had the trial but did not make the team. There were other officials watching the trials and one of them approached me and asked if I would be interested in signing up for his club.

He was from the Fiorentina Soccer Club which played in the Italian League of New York. Their home ground was at Dyker Park in Bensonhurst, Brooklyn. Since I lived only a couple of blocks from there, it seemed tailor-made for me.

Fiorentina Soccer Club, Dyker Park, Brooklyn

I was asked to come down to the club house on Kings Highway to sign the necessary papers and meet some of the players. I walked in the unmarked door of the club and into a room with men sitting at small tables. Some of them were sipping espresso and a few of them were playing dominoes, while others were just sitting around puffing on cigars. They all eyed me suspiciously. It was a scene instantly recognizable to any fan of a Scorsese mafia movie. However, the mood changed when the manager announced that I had just signed for the club. The men were soon smiling and shaking my hand. "Hey, welcome!" "Some anisette, eh?" "How about an espresso?"

I was now officially a member of the Fiorentina Club.

My early games with the club were a little difficult. Everyone was very welcoming but many of the members and players were relatively new immigrants and had difficulty with English. I was the only Brit playing in the Italian League. What on earth was I doing? I also soon found out that my British style of play was a lot more physical than that of my Mediterranean friends. This realization hit home during one of my first games when I tackled an opponent. He was waltzing down the touch-line with the ball at his feet. I hit him shoulder to shoulder, perfectly acceptable under the rules of the Football Association but it was just not done in the Italian League. He wasn't ready for the hit and went spinning over on his back. This led to a near riot. His team supporters, his family, and more notably his mother who was leading the charge, ran onto the field and chased after me at lightning speed.

Over my shoulder I could hear, "You animal! You try to killa my boy!" Eventually, order was restored, explanations were given (in Italian), and in my case, lessons learned.

I spent three very happy years with the Fiorentina club. The players and their families were very kind, and I became a celebrity of sorts as the only Englishmen in the league. And then in an Inter-Cup game against a team from another league, the Brooklyn Scots, I was in a tussle with one of their players who called me a "spaghetti-faced bastard." Obviously, an explanation was necessary, and we spoke after the game. He asked me to consider joining his Scottish team. I decided that my time with the Italians had run its course, and it was time for a change, especially to a British group.

Unfortunately, during my second season with the Brooklyn Scots, the club manager absconded with the club funds and the organization was disbanded.

I was then contacted by the manager of The Swedish Club of Bay Ridge, Brooklyn and was asked to sign for them. The Swedish Club only had two Swedes on the team, with the rest of the players being English, Irish and Scottish, with one Ecuadorean and two Italians. I had found my football home.

Our coach and manager was a man called Jackie Hynes. He was a member of the famous U.S.A. team that beat England in the World Cup in 1950. Jackie had roots in Scotland, and a passion for the game of soccer which he passed along to the players. He would eventually be inducted into the Soccer Hall of Fame.

Every home game my wife, Marion, would come with me, bringing our two children Robin and Adam who were only toddlers at the time. We would drive to the club in Bay Ridge. Marion would meet with the other wives and the kids found their playmates in the clubhouse. After the game we all socialized at the bar, with all the women chatting together and the players reliving the game. We made many friends, some of whom would last a lifetime. This all helped Marion and I to feel more at home in our still relatively new home country.

I stayed for seven years with the Swedish Club before moving to Ramsey, New Jersey. To finish up my football career, I played in an over-40 league. Eventually though, my injuries made me call it quits on the game that was so much a part of my life.

Jackie Hynes, Starlight Park, 1941

Swedish Club teammates Cameron
Ormiston and Hugh Dignon from
Glasgow, Scotland with Derek

Swedish Club teammates Dave
Saunders and Derek, 1971

Derek playing in Bay Ridge, 1968

A Pearl in New York

When my wife Marion and I arrived in New York after emigrating from our home in Liverpool, we were unemployed. It was a situation that had caused some consternation in our families as we prepared to leave.

Actually, as I tried to explain to them, it really wasn't quite as risky as it sounded. I had hedged our bet by having a little cash available to see us through a few weeks without work. I had also arranged interviews with a few insurance companies since I was a trained insurance underwriter when I arrived.

My cousin Nancy who was already living in Brooklyn had been sending me the job ads from the New York Times for a while, and I could see that there were many opportunities for an insurance underwriter with my experience. Just before we left, I had completed all my insurance exams and had been given an academic credential, so I felt very confident that I would find work without too much trouble.

I plunged into the interviews I had arranged before I left England. I was a little taken aback by the easy first name informality of these meetings. "Hey, Derek, nice to meet you. What do you think of America so far?" I also found that my designation, with letters after my name, for which I had worked so hard, did not account for much. Nobody had heard of the Royal Exchange, the professional body in England that had been around for two centuries, as had Lloyds of London, still the most famous name in insurance. I'll bet these Yanks think that they invented the insurance business like everything else in the world.

Soon I was able to swallow my pompous irritation at these insufferable Americans and decided that "when in America..."

In truth, I found this attitude of criticizing America and its ways to be quite prevalent amongst new immigrants. Everything is new and usually quite different than one's old country, so understandably there is some homesickness involved.

Unlike me, Marion embraced New York and America immediately. She loved the openness and informality of the people she met. There was no worrying about accent or class, so she felt very free and happy.

She would tell me, "Derek, pardon my stating the obvious, but if we wanted everything to be English then we should have stayed home." How dare people make so much sense? But her attitude helped me a great deal and I began to immerse myself into my new life.

My interviews went well, and I had a number of offers. However, some involved relocation, which was out of the question. There was one interview that went particularly well. It was with the Pearl / Monarch Insurance Company, the American branch of a large, wait for it......British company, the Pearl Assurance.

I was interviewed by the Executive Vice President which was most unusual since it was usually the Underwriting Manager after a screening by the Personnel Department. He was English and had seen my correspondence and resume. He was then asked to interpret my English designation and took an immediate interest in my situation in much more detail than usual. He had worked in senior positions in Canada and South Africa and seemed to run the show in the U.S. He wanted to know where I would live and about my family in Brooklyn. He became a mentor, although I did not know this at the time, perhaps because I didn't yet know what a mentor was.

His name was Gerald Heath. He answered the phone in a clipped English accent with "Heath here!" He was a heavy-set man and although somewhat affable, he did not smile a great deal. I quickly learnt to keep my jokes to myself.

I was then hired as an underwriter. The head of my department was Bill Bowden, a rather nervous, insecure individual which didn't bode well considering my special relationship, for that is what it became, with Mr. Gerald Heath.

My phone would ring and it would be Heath's secretary. "Mr. Heath would like to see you."

I would then go in to see Bill Bowden. "Bill, Mr. Heath has asked to see me." It was always "Mr. Heath."

"Anything wrong?" he would ask.

"Not as far as I'm concerned."

"Well, better get over there," he said through clenched teeth.

I had a few of these meetings with Heath. He wanted to know what I thought of the work, how were things at home, and how my wife was settling in. I rather enjoyed these sessions and was flattered that the big boss took such an interest me.

However, poor Bill Bowden didn't know what to make of it all. Here was this new kid, practically a trainee, having cozy one on one meetings with his boss, something that he would have loved but rarely had. Bowden probably thought that we were plotting his downfall and that Heath was bringing in a fellow Englishman to take over, as if I ever could. I could have explained that Heath was merely taking a friendly interest in me. I also could have mentioned the situation to Heath to make him aware. I did neither.

The other participants in the drama were my fellow underwriters. Three of them, in particular, had been very helpful and welcoming, not only with the work but in my New York life in general—navigating the subway, ordering lunch, going out for drinks, etc. These were relatively mundane tasks, but they seemed more challenging and different in this alien city. There were no signs in the subway, unlike the London Underground, and lunch was a series of multiple choices, much like a quiz show:

"I'd like a ham and cheese sandwich, please."

"What kind of bread? White? Rye? What kind of cheese? American? Swiss?"

And then there were the drinks. It was the early 1960's so it was Old Fashioneds, Manhattans, and Daiquiris. I would long for a good pint of ale. My head would be spinning not from the drinks but from all the choices and my co-workers thought it was so much fun. And it was.

Two of my co-workers were of German extraction. Ronnie Opperman, a hearty, exuberant, and overweight gentleman who would not have looked out of place in a Munich beer hall. The other was Charlie Henken, our supervisor, who was a tall, serious, blonde chap and more the S.S. officer type.

They too were curious about my special relationship with Heath but understood completely when I explained, but also agreed that I shouldn't approach Bowden on the subject.

It went on this way for just over a year when I received the offer of another position. The job was in a totally different kind of insurance, specialized and high risk, and much like the business experience I'd had in England. When I told Gerald Heath that I have been offered another position, he was not pleased. In fact, he was very disappointed and said that he had big plans for me. For instance, he had hoped that I would run the Pearl office in Washington D.C., which was news to me. He also said, and I remember his exact words: "You do realize that you will be painting on a much smaller canvas." He was right that the new market was just emerging and was very small, but to me that was the exciting challenge.

And so, I left the Pearl and the friendly, caring eye of Gerald Heath who had given me my start and for which I will always be grateful. As time went by our paths did cross again at meetings, conventions, etc. My company was successful in the new industry, and he was very happy for me, but it was obvious that he wished that I had stayed under his guidance at the Pearl.

CAREER MOVE

It was May, 1963 and Marion and I had been in the USA for almost eighteen months. We lived in an apartment in a two-family house in Flatbush, Brooklyn. She was pregnant with Robin, our first child, and had left her secretarial job at Remington Rand to join a temp agency, which gave her more flexibility during the pregnancy. At this point she was with a large life insurance agency in downtown Brooklyn as secretary to the owner, Joe Schulman, who had taken an avuncular interest in her.

One evening she said, "Mr. Schulman was asking me what you did, and when I told him about your insurance experience both here and in England, he became very interested and said that if ever you considered a change, that I should let him know."

Marion and I both knew that I did want a change. At the Pearl Monarch Insurance Company, I was an automobile underwriter and most of my time consisted of reviewing policies coming in from the other branches. There was no real examination of risk, and no challenge whatsoever.

Marion pursued this with her boss. A business colleague of his had an insurance brokerage office doing business with Lloyds of London. I did not know much about Lloyds, except the fact that they insured all types of insurance all over the world. Joe Schulman soon arranged for me to meet with the owners.

And so it was that at 6 p.m. one evening I found myself at 26 Court Street in downtown Brooklyn at the offices of B. and R. Excess Underwriters for an interview. As I waited, it occurred to me that I had done no research on this company. I was treating it as a friendly, casual reference rather than a possible career move. Too late now...

A blonde woman entered the room. "My name is Rose. I am Mr. Karlinsky's secretary. Please follow me." As we made our way to the president's office, I was struck by the rather grand furnishings that surrounded me—polished wooden desks adorned with fresh flowers, paintings on the wall, and thick carpeting. This was all in sharp contrast to my surroundings at the Pearl Assurance with its bare floors and steel desks.

As I entered Raymond Karlinsky's office I was quite taken aback to find four other people in the room besides Karlinsky. I later learned that this was his style. He craved an entourage. Even when commuting to the office he had a car full of people to talk to. I didn't know this at the time, and therefore found it difficult to understand why a twenty-nine year old junior insurance underwriter, and a new immigrant to boot, would warrant an interview with the CEO of the organization along with an array of executives.

Raymond Karlinsky was a huge man, over six feet tall and at least 250 pounds. I later learned that every year he went down to Duke University to undergo their "rice diet" treatment. He would come back looking, if not svelte, at least a little thinner. Needless to say, it didn't last.

Everyone introduced themselves and then kept quiet. Karlinsky then took over. "When you join us and get involved in what we do, you will never want to do anything else in this business." Wow. Sounded as though I had been hired even before the interview had begun! I later learned that this was just his style. He then launched into a colorful, enthusiastic description of what the firm did.

B. and R. Excess Corp was a large, wholesale insurance broker for Lloyd's of London. They handled large, difficult risks that came from other brokers mainly in the tri-state area who had no access to Lloyds. It was business that the standard insurance community would not write because of the unique or perhaps dangerous nature of the business.

During my interview Karlinsky asked, "Do you go to the theatre?"

"Yes, I do," I replied.

"Ever wonder what happens if the star of the show can't make the performance?"

Without waiting for my reply, he said, "Well let me tell you. The theatre loses money, so they buy a Non-Appearance policy from Lloyds through us in case that happens. Do you like rock n roll?"

Where is this going? I thought.

"Well, Lloyds insures concerts and artists. You wouldn't find Allstate doing that. Too many people, all kinds of problems if you have no history of controlling and pricing the risk. We and Lloyds together can do that."

He then described other exotic lines of insurance that they specialized in, but by then I was hooked. I felt like shouting "Where do I sign?!"

What impressed me was not only the type of insurance that Karlinsky was describing, but the enthusiasm he had for the business. He obviously loved it and I found that quite contagious.

The other executives in the room were partners in B. and R. and filled in details when called upon, but it was Karlinsky's show without a doubt. Each of them brought something quite different to the organization. Bill Malone was an Irishman with an office in Elizabeth, New Jersey where he cultivated a book of political business to send to Lloyds. Joe Neulinger was originally a Belgian diamond dealer with close ties to the diamond district in New York, which gave him business. Alan Quaif, an Englishman, was a former Underwriter at Lloyds, before Karlinksy persuaded him to come over to the USA. His contacts and knowledge of Lloyd's were invaluable. Last and perhaps least was Sam Neulinger, Joe's son, who was not a partner, but acted like one.

I was offered more money than I was earning at the Pearl, but hardly a dramatic increase, and was told to think about it. I couldn't wait to tell Marion, who agreed with me that it sounded like an exciting change and hopefully a good career move. I told B. and R. that I would be happy to join them.

Working at B. and R. was like no other office that I had worked in either in England or at the Pearl. There seemed to be no clear lines of authority or communication. I had understood that Alan Quaif was my boss, but he was always so harassed by Karlinsky that he hardly had time to field questions from me. Actually, everyone was harassed by Karlinsky. He would come out of his office yelling questions, demanding answers, and always probing. I do believe that he had forgotten our interview because he asked my name in that first week and asked if I had written any business.

I was responsible for assessing risks from brokers in New York to pass along to Lloyds and at the beginning I was quite bewildered not only by the risk selection, but at the pace and informality of the office. There was no formal training. I was given a desk and a phone and that was it. My savior was a man called Howie Liederman who had been with B. and R. for a while. He knew all the New York brokers and their sales tricks. I had a desk next to his and tried to enlist his help, which he offered cheerfully. At first, though, I was appalled at Howie's phone conversations:

"If you call again with this garbage, I swear I will cut you off! Call me when you get something halfway decent." He would then slam down the phone with a grin and say "He'll be back."

I thought of the insurance office in Liverpool where I had worked. Everyone called each other Mr., Mrs., and Miss during work hours, and it was all rather sedate. But this was another world entirely. Still, I had wanted a change and my goodness, did I get it. I started getting my own calls from brokers. Liability insurance on a new product or invention, a commercial fireworks display, an amusement park, a circus—all risks that regular companies would not touch and would usually be exported to London via our office.

I was just starting to get the feel of things when one day Alan Quaif called me into his office. "Do you know anything about handling claims?" he asked.

"No, I'm afraid not," I replied.

"Well, Terry McKeever our claims guy has pulled his back out and won't be in for a few weeks. We need you to handle the claims desk. Don't worry, we will help out."

Good luck with that, I thought, if the support and training was anything like my introduction to underwriting. But I had no choice and took over the claims desk. If the underwriting department was a challenge, then the claims desk was a trauma.

There were files scattered everywhere. I was to read through these, coordinate with Lloyds, and eventually receive authority to either pay or deny the claim. I didn't even know where to start.

Again, I had a savior, or rather two, in the form of my female assistants who had both been in the Claims Department for a long time. They led me through the morass of questions, bills, and various intricacies of dealing with Lloyds on claims. However, they could not save me from our own in-house attorneys, Kramer and Voletsky. All claims involving lawsuits were handled by this firm. It was incredibly lucrative since Karlinksky had arranged with Lloyds to agree to give them all the business with no competition from other firms. One would think that this would put them in a generally happy frame of mind. Far from it. Periodically, I could hear their shouts as they both marched along the corridor (they always came together) to my cubicle. They had a habit of waving the file or papers in question.

"Where is our money?" or "Why isn't this bill paid?" they'd shout at the top of their lungs.

"Let me check the status," I would say mildly.

"Status, status! We don't want the status, we want our money!"

If they had looked at each other and nodded emphatically it would have been pure Laurel and Hardy. At this point my lovely assistants would step in.

"I have something here from London. They have a payment on the way for this and other files. The draft will be here tomorrow."

"Well, it's about time! Cut the checks as soon as the funds come in," they would grumble, storming away down the hall.

It was an office culture that took me a while to get used to, but eventually I did. The group of people I worked with were smart and incredibly focused, the latter being something that perhaps I had not experienced before.

The business we were in was a dynamic, rapidly growing segment of insurance that I had been lucky enough to stumble upon, thanks to Marion. With a number of twists and turns, it was to engage me for the next thirty years of my life.

PART 4

RISKY BUSINESS

It was November, 1967. I had been in Miami for just five months and things had been going rather well. In June I had been transferred down from New York by my employer there to our newly acquired company, State Fire and Casualty Insurance Company. This was a sleepy provincial company writing local auto and homeowner's insurance in the state of Florida. My assignment was to begin distribution of large commercial insurance on difficult and unusual risks, an aspect of the business I had been involved in with Lloyds of London during my four years in New York. The reception from the intermediaries in Florida and other southern states had been excellent, and distribution of the new products was going very well. Even more importantly, my wife Marion and I along with our two small children were enjoying our new experience in the state of Florida. The company had given me a car and we had rented a small house in North Miami. Life was good.

Derek with son Adam, daughter Robin, and wife Marion, 1967

I was sitting at the desk in my office when my secretary appeared in the doorway.

"Mr. Gumpert wants to see you in his office right away."

Stanley Gumpert, President of State Fire and Casualty Co. often asked to see me, to discuss one thing or another, however there was an urgency about this that was a little unusual.

I hurried over and was ushered into his very large office. He was sitting behind a mahogany desk that seemed to stretch the length of the room and whose top was covered in glass with a variety of seashells underneath befitting our Miami, Florida location.

Stanley Gumpert was a thin, nervous man who, even when he smiled, still looked rather anxious. He wasn't smiling now and was indeed anxious.

He stood up and came around the desk.

"Derek, I don't quite know how to put this, so I will come right to the point. I would advise you to immediately begin looking for a position elsewhere."

I could not believe what I had just heard.

"I'm sorry, Mr. Gumpert, but I don't understand. Is it my work? I thought things were going extremely well."

"If it is any comfort, you are doing an excellent job but I'm afraid I'm not at liberty to say any more than that," he said. "I'm telling you this only because I feel somewhat responsible for bringing you and your family down here from New York."

As well he might. He had been insistent on having some New York large risk expertise in his office and had requested me for the new operation. Still, I had been flattered as it was a great opportunity and I had accepted, so I could hardly blame him.

So now here I was on the verge of losing my job, goodness knows why, with a wife and two small children, away from my base in New York. I left Mr. Gumpert's office feeling sick to my stomach.

I immediately called my colleagues in the New York office and some industry contacts to see if they knew anything. Everyone was mystified. When I went home and told Marion, she was remarkably calm about the whole thing.

"Whatever the reason, you are still a known quantity in the business and if they don't want you, others will."

Ah, yes, but will they? I was still very anxious about my future and my ability to take care of the family. I broke out in hives and couldn't sleep. I was putting feelers out, but nothing was happening,

Then I began getting calls telling me that the word on the street was that my employer in New York was in serious financial trouble, but there were no details. So that was it.

I felt somewhat better that it was a corporate problem and not of my doing. Then, a stroke of luck. Our industry convention would be held in two weeks' time at the iconic luxury Hotel Fontainebleau in Miami Beach, practically in my backyard. I could not afford the fees required to register but I could use the lobby and the bars to meet up with old friends and contacts in my quest for a new position.

During that convention week I was at the Fontainebleau every day and every evening. The picture on the New York company had clarified somewhat. The principals were all under indictment and there was talk of a RICO prosecution. I worried that this could affect my job prospects. After all, I had worked with these people. Luckily, I was never made an officer, which would have happened at the end of the year, so I was not named in the lawsuits. Still, it made for some uncomfortable introductions to people who did not know me.

I was still lobbying after a few days with a few possibilities, but not really finding what I was looking for. There was an opportunity to join an agency in Shreveport, Louisiana, a broker's office in Fort Lauderdale and a reinsurance firm in Tampa. But I soon realized that what I really needed was to get back to New York, the place where I had started, and back to my friends and family.

Enter Len Englehardt, from lobby left. He approached me one morning in the lobby of the Fontainebleau. "So I hear that you worked with those crooks in New York who are being indicted?"

I soon learned that this was Len's approach—always get the first punch in and put your opponent on the defensive, because to Len, everyone in business was an opponent until he decided otherwise. Of course, I didn't know him then. He was just a New York broker who had been around for a very long time. He told me that people at the convention had suggested we get together. Len was a small ruddy faced man who did not stand on ceremony.

We talked for a very long time over coffee during which he told me that he was starting a special risk company with capital from a family in Brazil who had banking and insurance interests in Latin America and wanted a presence in the U.S. Len had been introduced to these people by a lawyer friend. He told me, frankly, that he was not a company man, he was an insurance broker who had been in New York for years but knew nothing about running a company.

He had agreed to organize the company and in return he would use it exclusively in New York for his brokerage business. The company was already licensed but doing almost no business. They had a small staff but needed marketing and underwriting expertise. A number of people, knowing my situation and my background, had suggested that Len talk to me.

I liked Len. In business he was rough, tough and pulled no punches. For years afterwards people marveled at how well we worked together: the prissy Englishman joining forces with the street fighter broker from Brooklyn. But we did. He liked that I did not roll over on his decisions as others did. I pushed back on the bombast that usually terrified many other people. During our sometimes heated discussions (Len despised any other kind), I left plenty of room for his dignity and pride. Besides, he was an unabashed Anglophile, spending as much time as he could in London. Obviously, that was hardly a disadvantage as far as I was concerned.

It was the beginning of, if not a beautiful friendship, then certainly a long and profitable association and a business career that I could hardly have imagined during those dark few weeks in Miami in November, 1967.

LUCKY OR SMART?

It was May 1972. Marion and I were sitting with our drinks on the balcony of our suite at the Copacabana Hotel in Rio de Janeiro, Brazil looking out over Guanabara Bay. Later a car would be picking us up to take us to the chairman's house for a dinner in our honor.

A month earlier I had been appointed President and CEO of Western World Insurance Company which was owned by the Chairman, Antonio de Larragoiti and his Brazilian/ Argentine family. At that board meeting he had insisted that Marion and I travel to Rio to meet the other major stockholders. So here we were.

"Don't you feel that there is something slightly surreal about all of this?" Marion asked.

"Actually, I was just about to break into a rendition of "If They Could See Me Now," I replied, sipping on my Brazilian caipirinha cocktail.

We had good reason to pinch ourselves. It was only four years earlier that I had joined Western World Insurance Company in Newark, New Jersey, with its focus on difficult and unusual insurance risks.

Len and I had worked closely together over the next three years building the company, and I assumed more and more responsibility while Len concentrated on his own brokerage business. Our management styles were quite different, but we worked together splendidly. After losing his temper with someone, Len would turn to me and say, "I know you don't approve of the way I handled that. Well, too bad, that's the way I do things." That was as close to an apology as Len could get.

It was in December, 1971 when Len announced to me that he was retiring, and that he would be proposing to the Board of Directors in April at the Annual General Meeting that I would take over the position of President and CEO.

I had been with Western World for only 4 years, I was 37 years old, and I didn't feel at all ready for the top job, the ultimate responsibility. Besides that, Len thoroughly enjoyed being CEO. It gave him a stature in the industry that he never had as a street broker. Why give it up?

As we spoke in depth later, I learned that as we were growing into a sizable organization he did not want the worry and responsibility. Besides, he was feeling his age. He was in his late 60's.

Len then told me, "I have spoken to Antonio and he and the stockholders have given it their blessing."

Over the next few months, Len did a thorough job of making our various constituencies aware of the change. I began to feel more comfortable, but it was still sometimes difficult to believe that this was happening just ten years after arriving in the U.S.

Was I smart or was I lucky?

From left: Derek with brothers Robert, Cyril, Bill, and Stan

During my frequent trips to England and Switzerland to our reinsurers, who shared the burden of risk with us, I always took time to spend a weekend in Liverpool. I would get together with my four brothers and my youngest sister Dorothy, and their families. Amongst the well-wishers who were happy for me and my progress in the U.S. ("we're very proud of you," "you've done very well," etc.) there was always the not so still, not so small voice of my younger brother, Cyril.

"Our Derek was always lucky. I'll tell you one thing, he was no bloody genius, that I can remember. One minute he's out of work, then he meets a feller with a plum job to offer. Don't tell me that's not luck."

He had a point, but it was not something that I needed to ponder, and certainly not on that lovely evening in Rio. Anyway, there's the car. Better get going.

Charles (Len) Engelhardt with Derek, newly appointed President and
CEO of Western World Insurance Company, 1972

AULD LANG SYNE

Growing up in Liverpool in the 1940's and 1950's, celebrating the New Year was an important rite of passage. "Christmas is for the kids, but New Year is for us," was the refrain from the adults as they drank and danced the New Year in. At midnight the streets would be filled with people singing "Auld Lang Syne" and wishing each other the best for the year to come.

And then there were the good luck rituals. On the stroke of midnight, the family would arrange for a dark-haired person, family or neighbor, to walk in the door. They would be carrying a lump of coal for warmth, a piece of bread for food, and some money. These were all good omens for the year ahead. They would then leave with some ashes to symbolize the end of the old year.

For the young people, it meant the biggest dance of the year, lasting until midnight. The pubs stayed open late and despite the inevitable overindulgence, we always had a grand time.

For a few years in the 1950's I was working at the Westminster Bank, and in those days every ledger and cashier's till had to be balanced on the last day of the year. No one could go home until it was done. Sometimes just a five-pound error would keep us there frantically searching until it was finally found. I would constantly be checking my watch, fretting over all the lost drinking and dancing time. Don't these people realize that it's New Year's Eve, for goodness sake?? When we finally finished balancing the books, I would jump on the bus and race to the dance hall, ready to make up for lost time.

For the first few years in Brooklyn, Marion and I were too busy settling into our new life and starting a family to worry about New Year rituals.

But upon returning to New Jersey from Miami, Marion and I started having New Year's Eve celebrations at our small garden apartment in Plainfield. It was a start for sure, but certainly not the kind of British "knees-up" we both had in mind.

Then came our move to Ramsey, New Jersey and our first house. Built on the site of an old grist mill, it was a very large, three story, fieldstone house overlooking a beautiful, secluded acre of land. This was ideal for parties both inside and out. It was April of 1972 and by the end of the year we were quite settled. We decided to throw our first New Year's Eve party in our new house.

It was to be the first of many New Year's Eve bashes, lasting nearly twenty years, with the same core group and cast of characters. Like many immigrants, we tended to gravitate to the expat community. My soccer team included a number of Brits who became close friends. I also had my Liverpool family who had settled in the states: my cousin Nancy who sponsored our immigration, Nancy's brother Don and his wife Emily who also emigrated to the U.S. from Liverpool, as well as my sister Angela and her husband Malcolm (Mac) who had also settled here.

Over the years we had many additions, including neighbors and business colleagues, but the British core group was always the same. Most of my soccer friends were blue collar workers, although one, a Scotsman from

Glasgow named Hugh Dignon, was an English professor at Queens College. Hugh was our blue collar academic.

From left: Derek, Hugh Dignon, brother-in-law Malcom McLeod (Mac), and Dave Saunders

In other words, it was not your usual affluent, American suburban group. In fact, it was quite the opposite. No one had anything to prove, no one cared where you worked or how much money you made. You were there to dance and sing, and overall have a bloody good time. And, indeed, we always did.

The evening usually started with the arrival of my best friend, Dave Saunders and his wife Karen. I met Dave while playing soccer in Brooklyn for the Swedish Club, and he would become godfather to my youngest daughter Jenny who was born a year after we moved to the new house.

The two would come early to help set up the bar and all the food. I can still picture this wonderful scene—my wife Marion and his wife Karen in our bedroom, sitting together at the dresser in front of the mirror, laughing, gossiping, and getting ready, each with a vodka and tonic in hand.

The evening would start with drinks as people arrived and chatted with one another. I was always the disc jockey and some slow mood music was the order of the day at that point in the evening. As the evening progressed, there would always be some sing-alongs, which was usually Irish folk music like the Clancy Brothers and of course, The Beatles. At around 10 p.m., Marion would lay out the buffet on the dining table, away from the party area. This would be the opportunity for people to slow down a little on the drinking and do their "party-pieces," which was usually a song from the old country, a dance, or a comedy monologue. My cousin Don was a master of the latter and could recite all of the English comedian Stanley Holloway's pieces by heart.

Then it was time for the party to kick into high gear and I would pull out all the stops with music blasting from the stereo, and soon the house would reverberate with the sounds of "YMCA" and "I Wanna Hold Your Hand." A large circle of dancing revelers began to form, churning up a frenzy of foot-stomping, hand-clapping, gleeful singing, and cackling laughter that would literally make the walls and the floor shake, pulse and pound right along with the beat. Hence the Liverpool expression for a fun, raucous party – a "knees-up."

It was at this point that I handed out a succession of party hats whose style deviated from the traditional New Year's Eve headwear. Among the hats of choice were the following: an authentic British Bobby Hat, a purple, rakish, heavily-plumed hat that would have made the Three Musketeers envious, a Spanish matador hat, a yellow construction hard hat, a Turkish fez, and a soldier's helmet from the Zulu wars, among others. It was a wonderful opportunity for everyone to look rather silly which was the whole point. Dignity and decorum had both left the building some time ago.

At the stroke of midnight it was time to make the circle for "Auld Lang Syne" which nobody sings more fervently than my Scottish friends, although I do wish they would not insist on singing all of the verses.

Of course, it was inevitable that at that kind of party, alcohol would play a part. On the positive side, shy people lost their inhibitions to dance and sing without a care, but on the flip side we did have to worry about our guests drinking and driving. For the most part it would be the designated driver approach (which was usually the wife), but we also had to insist on people staying overnight, sleeping on chairs and sofas. In all the years of our New Year's Eve parties, we never had a serious drinking incident, whether it be a fight or a driving accident. But then again that could have been sheer luck.

And yes, the parties did get loud and the neighbors who weren't invited did sometimes call the police, but it was a relatively small town, and the cops were usually quite understanding about it all.

Our New Year's Eve celebrations carried on year after year for almost twenty years. It was a periodic reminder of our home in England, which after so many years should not have been necessary but, to so many immigrants, it usually is.

These parties were like a successful, long-running Broadway musical that somehow still managed to retain its fun and exuberance despite the number of performances.

It was a little touch of Liverpool in the night.

Pre-party, New Year's Eve,
1985

Cousin Nancy, Derek, and Marion,
New Year's Eve, 1979

Family photo in backyard of
Ramsey house, 1974

Brother-in-law Malcom McLeod
(Mac) and friend Mitch Gwinn,
New Year's Eve, 1983

LAST DAYS

I entered our house in Ramsey, New Jersey on that Thursday in April, 1995 and shouted Marion's name (actually, "Mal," which was my nickname for her) to announce that I was home. There was no answer. I figured she must be out. Then I remembered that she had had an appointment for her annual mammogram procedure.

I went upstairs to change my clothes and, as I approached the bedroom, I heard her crying inside. I opened the door, and she ran across the room and flung herself into my arms.

"What on earth is the matter"? I asked.

She told me between sobs that they had found a lump on her breast and that they had double checked and there was no mistake.

Marion was a petite, blonde, pretty woman. At that point we had been together for 40 years. We had two daughters, one who was recently married, and a son. Ours was a long and loving relationship.

We sat and talked. I took the optimistic view that yes, there was a lump, but it may not be a major problem or even cancerous. Marion was more realistic and said that from her discussions with the doctor it looked serious enough that he suggested immediate discussion with an oncologist.

To further complicate matters we were leaving the next day to spend a weekend in Burlington, Vermont for our youngest daughter Jenny's graduation from the University of Vermont. We were meeting my sister and her husband and another friend, Jenny's godfather Dave Saunders and his wife Josephine up there.

Marion already had the names of three oncologists in New York. We called from various payphones on our six hour drive to Vermont in hopes of securing doctor appointments, but none were available.

Thus began a sort of charade. We did not want to cast a pall over what should have been a lovely, joyous occasion. Jenny wanted us to meet the parents of her friends and to make a party out of the weekend. We decided to go along with it and not even mention our problem to my sister or our friends. We were determined to act as though we did not have a care in the world, and to make this a wonderful time for our daughter. After the graduation ceremony we all went out together to a local restaurant to celebrate.

Marion was just wonderful—chatting with the parents, laughing with Jenny and her friends, drinking a vodka and tonic…She played her part to the hilt. There were times when I looked at her and almost convinced myself that the whole thing about the mammogram hadn't happened, and that everything was just fine. But then we would catch each other's eye and see the anxiety, knowing this was but a temporary respite on the daunting journey that lay ahead.

We eventually decided upon a Dr. Garrett at Columbia Presbyterian Hospital in New York. He was an affable, low-key individual with a fine reputation.

At this point and for a long time afterwards I regarded Marion's breast cancer as something of a temporary setback and, with surgery and treatment, all would be well again. This attitude flew in the face of all the medical evidence which indicated an aggressive, virulent cancer which would inevitably spread.

Marion was not in denial, but she was hopeful that by bringing all of the medical and even non-medical resources to bear on the disease she could, if not be cured, at least keep the beast at bay.

When our friends and family heard the news we were given the usual anecdotal evidence indicating that we had nothing to worry about. "My friend at work had breast cancer and after radiation she was fine," and "You would be surprised at the number of women who have survived breast cancer. I wouldn't worry," etc.

At this stage, just a month or two after the diagnosis, she was fine. She was socializing with family and friends, going into New York for theatre and dinner, and all seemed well.

On the next visit with Dr. Garrett, he recommended a mastectomy, which was performed soon afterwards. The slow descent had begun. The mastectomy brought us even closer together. Marion was brave and worried more about me than herself, even in the face of this medical assault. We clung to each other for whatever comfort we could find. She lost her hair after the chemo, and she laughed about us looking more and more like each other.

Then began the twice weekly visits to Columbia Presbyterian for chemotherapy, and I would join her on the visits. Marion welcomed the treatments. She would say that she could sit there and will the chemo to destroy the cancer cells and make her well again. Afterwards we would celebrate with a long lunch and a drink, although on that point, Marion was a little anxious: "Dr. Garrett, Derek and I will be having lunch. Is it okay for me to have a vodka and tonic without spoiling the effect of the chemo?"

Garrett would smile and say, "Have as many as you like. In fact, have one for me." He knew.

It was during these post chemo celebrations that I was actually fooled into believing that all was right again. Still, relief and hope were in the air if only temporarily.

We were now into 1996. We were spending more and more time in New York with visits to Dr. Garrett, chemo treatments and Marion's group therapy sessions with other cancer patients. We decided to rent an apartment in New York. We had always loved the city and came in often, so now it really made sense to have a place here.

We settled on a rented apartment in the Olympic Tower on 51st and Fifth Avenue. It had floor to ceiling windows with views all the way up Fifth Avenue. I remember when we first saw it and Marion said, "One day this could be your bachelor pad." It was a joking remark but it thoroughly frightened me, since it showed what Marion was really thinking. Looking back, I realize that being the kind of person she was with her wise, realistic view of life she would have wanted a frank discussion of her illness and where we were headed. But she was compassionate enough to know that I couldn't handle it and wanted to spare me, despite her indication that one day I would be alone.

We began to enjoy our New York life despite it being centered around doctor visits and treatments. However, if I became too optimistic and hopeful and encouraged Marion to be the same, Marion would offer the sobering remark "Derek, there are two kinds of people in the world—those who have cancer and those who do not." Or "Derek, I have Stage 4 cancer. There is no Stage 5."

She was in no way feeling sorry for herself. It was her way of trying to get me to look at the situation realistically and get me out of my cocoon of denial. However, in her own way she was also hopeful, and she showed this in her pursuit of possible cures. She was constantly searching and talking to people whom she thought might be able to help. She also worked with an energy healer, tried acupuncture, and even worked with a quack doctor (there is no other word for him) who offered injections that were of no use at all. Marion would check all of this out with Dr. Garrett, whose reply was always that it couldn't do any harm, which to me spoke volumes. As for me, even though I was really quite skeptical of these attempts at a cure, I would never have dissuaded her from trying them if it gave her hope and made her feel as though at least she was doing something.

Marion had obtained her Masters in Social Work as an adult student and was interested in the work of Carl Jung and had always wanted to visit the Carl Jung Institute in Switzerland. She knew of a seminar coming up in July and asked Dr. Garrett if it would be okay for her to travel to it. He agreed, provided I came along, which I certainly intended to.

The week was far more interesting for Marion than it was for me but I enjoyed being there with her as she attended lectures and discussion groups and loved it all. We had spent the week before touring and visiting friends in Zurich and having a wonderful time. I was sure that she was in remission.

Then it all came to a grinding halt. One day near the end of the week at the Institute, Marion said that she had to speak to Dr. Garrett since something was wrong. She suddenly felt ill. He told her to get home immediately.

We then saw Dr. Garrett on our return and received the news that the cancer had spread to Marion's lungs. She would need an oxygen tank to help with her breathing. I also noted that Marion's deterioration showed in Dr. Garrett's attitude. He was so much more solemn in his discussions with us. This would have seemed to be the time to ask how long Marion had to live but we never did, although I think Marion always knew or had a good guess. I didn't want to know.

This was now the fall of 1996 and although we tried to keep up the New York life, theatre, church etc, it became more and more difficult. Marion spent more time in bed resting where she would receive friends and family, as well as the constant phone calls from our family in England. She still kept up her brave, wise face through it all. I clung to my cowardice and refused to face the obvious.

Derek, Marion, and (from left) daughter Jenny, son Adam, and eldest daughter Robin in Sea Isle City, NJ, 1996

During the fall we spent time at our condo on the Jersey shore which was right on the ocean. She had always enjoyed the water and felt that it was good for her spiritually and gave her strength. We were also joined by friends and family. Marion seemed so happy.

As 1996 was coming to an end we talked about New Year's Eve. Marion wanted to do something special.

We loved Irish music and had a favorite Irish band, The Clancy Brothers and Tommy Makem. Tommy Makem had a bar on 57th and Lexington and Marion insisted on going there early in the evening to have a drink and listen to some music. We had a lovely time with all kinds of memories brought back by the songs. We could hardly see the New Year in but left happy enough early in the evening.

It was early in 1997 and very cold. By this time Marion was in a wheelchair but still loved to go out in the cold weather. She had always enjoyed brisk, energizing walks around our Ramsey neighborhood, and long, blustery treks on the beach in the middle of winter. She seemed to thrive on it. All the more reason for us to venture outside in the cold and make our way around the streets near Rockefeller Center.

One Sunday the area was almost deserted and as we were going by the ice rink, we saw a film crew shooting on the steps. As we came closer, we saw that the person being filmed was one of our favorite English actresses, Julie Walters.

"Let's stay and watch, there's nobody here," said Marion. "But would you get me a hot chocolate?" As I left her, I saw that Ms. Walters was now alone. The film crew were huddling away from her and there she stood, a lone figure at the top of the steps. I decided to approach her.

"Ms.Walters, I'm getting a hot chocolate for my wife, would you like one?"

"Ooh, thanks love, it's bloody freezing here!" she replied.

I came back with the drinks but by this time Julie Walters was surrounded by the film crew again. I kept her chocolate and waited. However, she never did get free again and I drank it myself.

"I wonder if Julie Walters will tell people in England how this guy promised her a hot drink on a freezing cold day and never followed through? And will she think badly of all New Yorkers because of me?"

"I wouldn't worry too much about that if I were you," Marion said dryly.

On the night of Sunday, February 16th Marion was quite agitated. I was sitting with her in the bedroom. She was in bed and complaining that she was too hot. I had turned off the heat in the room, but she insisted that heat was getting through. She tossed and turned but could not get comfortable. She asked me to have the maintenance man come up to check the pipes. He did and said that all the heat was off.

She eventually went to sleep and so did I. At around 4 a.m. I awoke to a strange stillness in the room.

I switched on the light to look at Marion. She lay as though asleep but when I checked she was not breathing.

I remember being very frightened. I kept checking her breathing and pulse, refusing to believe what I knew to be true.

I then called 911 and waited, lying on the bed next to Marion. I heard the siren of the ambulance and jumped up. I could see all the way up a deserted Fifth Avenue as the ambulance came into view with lights flashing and siren blaring.

I turned to Marion. "Don't worry love, the ambulance will be here in a minute."

**Marion and Derek with son Adam
at Pontin's Holiday Camp, 1979**

**Marion and Derek with daughter
Robin at her wedding, 1994**

**Marion graduating with honors
from Fordham University with a
Masters in Social Work**

**Marion with daughter Jenny at her
college graduation, 1995**

AFTERMATH

My wife Marion died on the morning of President's Day, February, 17th, 1997.

I had called the EMT people and as they busied themselves around me, I sat as though in a dream, but somehow was able to snap to when it came to answering their questions.

Then came the NYPD: two cops who came up to my apartment on the 31st floor of the Olympic Tower, at the corner of 51st and Fifth Avenue. They expressed their condolences, asked about my family, and engaged me congenially in general conversation. It was only later that I learned that they were there, in fact, to quietly detain me until Marion's oncologist had been contacted to officially confirm her condition and cause of death. I was a suspect until proven otherwise. Marion would have smiled at that one.

The funeral arrangements and the arrival of my family from England kept my mind off things to some extent. It seemed at times that Marion and I were attending to the details of an event, the kind of thing we had done so many times before. This time, however, we were never in the same room together.

After the funeral, everyone went back to their lives and left me to mine, such as it was. Soon I was bombarded with phone calls from family and friends.

"How are you feeling?"

"Are you eating?"

"I hope you are getting out."

I would give reassuring answers but what I really wanted to say was "Whatever" or "Who cares?" That was the way I felt—just a total indifference at that point.

The only time I felt anything approaching engagement with life was from a most unlikely source. It was my attendance at a Shakespeare class at the New School. I had enrolled a semester earlier at Marion's insistence. I was constantly hovering over her, and she wanted time to herself. We both selected the Shakespeare class which I hadn't studied for years and soon I was enjoying the course and discussing it with her.

After her death I continued with the class more enthusiastically than ever. All the ingredients of my condition—love, loss, death, and despair—were right there in his tragedies. Hamlet, Macbeth, Lear, Othello…I immersed myself and found a strange comfort, although no answers, in these plays.

It did however prove to be a temporary respite from what felt like time spent sleepwalking through this new life I was leading.

Soon came the inevitable and well-meaning introductions…

"I'd like you to meet this lovely lady who lost her husband recently."

"I have this friend who you would really enjoy. Just someone to talk to or go to the movies with…"

"I'll arrange a dinner and you can meet this friend of mine."

All of these accompanied by "This is just for company, of course. We just don't want to see you alone."

But this was the last thing I needed. I didn't want to socialize or even talk to people, especially strangers, no matter how well-meaning they were. I didn't even answer the phone unless I felt it absolutely necessary. Eventually, though, I didn't have the energy to refuse. I finally acquiesced to these requests for various introductions.

Those poor women.... I can't remember a single face (except for the divorced mother of one of my daughter's friends, whom I had met before.) The encounters, such as they were, remain a vague, hazy memory. In all of these meetings there was never a question, on my part anyway, of sex or even affection. This was not surprising since I found even basic conversation difficult.

I remember one woman who booked a table at La Grenouille, one of the premier French restaurants in New York City. Not only did she reserve the table but she ordered for us both whilst carrying on an animated conversation with the maitre d' in French. She then paid the bill. Normally, I would have found that to be quite impressive. But again, it was one of my "whatever" moments. I didn't even ask her up to my apartment. As I look back, I really am appalled at my behavior at that time. I would drift through drinks and dinner and then could not wait to get back to the quiet of my apartment

I was still attending church services at Saint Thomas Episcopal church on Fifth Avenue. A few weeks after Marion's death I was listening to a sermon by a guest preacher, the Bishop of New York. In it he mentioned that he had recently lost his wife. The next day I called his office and told him that I had heard him speak and told him of Marion's death. He invited me to visit him at his office at The Cathedral of Saint John the Divine.

We talked about the loss of our wives and how we were handling the grieving. He talked about the value of a quiet, reflective time and the difficulty of achieving that. He mentioned a convent, the Community of the Holy Spirit, just an hour from New York. It was run by Episcopal nuns and available for retreats. I seized on this and soon was in touch with the convent to arrange for some time there.

I was to have a room at the convent with no time limit, and payment was at my discretion. Soon I was in the office of the sister in charge and taken to my room. It was very small, with a desk, a bed and a small bookcase stocked with reading on religion and philosophy. I had also brought my own book supply.

The rules were quite simple. I was on my own but could eat with the sisters, observing the rule of silence. I could attend the church services during the day and evening, or not, if I so chose. If I wanted to eat in my room, I could pick up some food at the main house. The sisters were not interested in why I was on the retreat, but if I wanted to talk to them, that was fine too. This more than suited me. At long last I had the chance to be by myself, with no phone calls or interruptions. It was an opportunity for reflection, and for introspection. I needed to look at what lay ahead, without the person who had been so much of my life for over forty years.

I found the sisters to be very matter-of-fact in their duties around the convent, and they all had jobs to do. Sometimes at Evensong and Vespers I would join in the service and loved to hear them sing. During the two weeks or so that I was there, I did not share too many meals with them. I found the silence a little disconcerting and getting possession of the salt without speaking was sometimes a little tricky.

The food left a lot to be desired: lots of salads (there was a working farm on the property) but not well-prepared. Chicken was also popular, but goodness knows what they did with it. Obviously, the idea was to shed not only our cares and woes, but also a few pounds. However, I understood that the sisters were really too busy with the maintenance and administration to think too much about creature comforts for their guests, me being the only one.

I spent my time reading, thinking and walking around the countryside that surrounded the convent. I never engaged in conversation with the sisters unless it involved housekeeping details. This arrangement suited us both.

On the first Sunday I was approached by the sister in charge who told me that if I wished to join them for morning service in Brewster, the local town, I was quite welcome.

"Don't worry about transportation—the sisters will have a car and you can join them. Sister Mary will be the designated driver."

My first thought was that this meant that Sister Mary would be having less of the communion wine than her companions. Actually, it just meant that she was our chauffeur.

As I sat in the passenger seat next to Sister Mary, I realized that this outing in the car meant a lot to her. She had a sly smile on her face as she rode the curves and bends of the countryside around Brewster, and then brought the car to a stop with a rather dramatic flourish outside the church.

The sisters made their entrance into the church in single file, from a side door and sat in the special pew in the front of the church with me in the middle. I could feel the respect of the congregation for the sisters and I felt rather proud to be there with them.

Soon I began to realize that it was time to get back to my life—friends, family, and whatever lay ahead. I then made arrangements to go back to New York.

There were no tearful goodbyes, which was understandable given my time with the sisters in those two weeks. Just a word from the nun in charge that I was always welcome should I ever wish to come back.

I did not come away from my spiritual retreat filled with joy and contentment. But I did feel a glimmer of hope, and I was certainly in a better place than I was before my time at the convent.

HELLO HELEN

It was February 17th, 1998, the first anniversary of Marion's death. It had been a very difficult year. I felt that I had lived it in a sort of fog.

I was still active in business, serving on the Board of Directors for Western World, the company from which I had retired. I also served on the board of the Shakespeare Society and The Gilbert and Sullivan Players. These were the only times I felt anywhere near animated.

Socially, however, I was totally out of it. I wanted nothing to do with anyone outside of my very close friends and family circle, and I wasn't even too sure about them.

I was still living in the Olympic Tower on 51st and Fifth Avenue, and from my high floor apartment with its floor to ceiling windows, I was able to play the rather depressed monarch of all I surveyed.

On this particular day I decided to venture out in the very early evening, but not very far. I walked out of the back of my building down to the bar of the Omni Berkshire Hotel on the corner of 52nd and Madison Avenue. The bar was surprisingly empty for the cocktail hour. I sat down at the bar and ordered a vodka martini, straight up, with large olives. Through my body language I made it clear to the bartender that I was not interested in conversation of any kind and could care less how the New York Giants or anyone else had fared that day. I was becoming an expert in the nuances of antisocial behavior. I gave off a sort of scent in that regard.

I sat there quietly, lost in my thoughts when I heard a voice say, "My mother used to drink those."

I looked up and saw an attractive blonde woman in a red business suit holding a briefcase. She was not looking at me but at the martini glass on the bar.

"My mother loved martinis with large olives," she continued wistfully, finally shifting her gaze to me.

"W-W-Would you like one?" I stuttered, rather than offered.

"Thank you, I will. I am meeting someone although he is very late."

Her colleague, whom I found out later had his wires crossed, never did arrive.

Her name was Helen and her mother had died a couple of months ago. She was feeling the loss very keenly. I told her about Marion and soon we were talking about death, grief, loss, and loneliness—all the wonderful subjects that are the prelude to romance.

Ironically, I felt happier, engaged and more relaxed than I had been in a long time. Of course, the martinis helped, because I did have another. Or was it two?

"Would you like to have dinner with me?" I asked hesitantly.

Unlike me, Helen did not seem at all intimidated by the situation. "I am hungry, yes, thank you."

We went to a stylish Italian restaurant next to the Olympic Tower and continued to talk. She had her own executive recruiting business and lived on the Upper East Side. She had grown up on the Philadelphia "Main Line" in an affluent family, her late mother being part of the Gretz beer family of Philadelphia. Helen had been divorced for a number of years and had four sons. She had also lived in Egypt for two years. An interesting lady indeed...

Helen had asked me about living in the Olympic Tower, so I asked her if she would like to see my apartment, carefully avoiding any mention of etchings. She agreed and we went up. After taking in the views from the various windows and looking remarkably unimpressed, she sat on the edge of a chair with her large coat clutched tightly in her hands, obviously poised for flight (although I didn't see it that way at the time). We talked for a little while longer and exchanged phone numbers. I then saw her to the elevator, gave her a peck on the cheek, and she was gone.

One would have thought that having had one of the most interesting evenings in a long time I would have called her, but I did not. I preferred instead to retreat back into my shell and be alone as much as possible.

One day the phone rang. A voice tentatively asked, "Is this Derek"?

"Yes, it is. Who is this?"

"This is Helen Rauch. We met a few weeks ago."

Helen's recollection is that at this point all she heard from my end was "Ohhh..."

She continued, undeterred.

"I've just returned from a business trip to London. I remembered you were English, and I thought I would say hello and bring you greetings from England."

We chatted about the theatre and the show she saw in London, and I asked if she would like to see the play "Art."

Helen said she would, so I began to make arrangements.

COURTING MS. HELEN

On my first evening out with Helen, we arranged to meet for pre-theatre dinner at Barbetta's, a rather opulent Italian place on Restaurant Row on 48th Street and 8th Avenue. I arrived early so that I could watch for her coming in the door.

As I sat there in the almost empty restaurant, I heard the waiters who were standing nearby, discussing the upcoming World Cup Soccer Championships and giving their opinions on the various teams. Being a lad from Liverpool, where soccer is in our veins, I couldn't help joining in and discussing the merits of the various teams. They were delighted at the banter, and brought over the maître d' to join in. Luckily, I looked up in time to see this lovely blonde woman in a black coat with a fur collar, walk in the door. It was Helen. She looked around the room and I stood up to wave to her. She gave me a big smile and gestured toward the cloak-room. Soon she was back looking happy and relaxed, just as I was. Meanwhile my soccer loving Italian waiters smothered us with so much attention that Helen couldn't fail to be impressed.

It continued on this happy note. We went to the theatre after dinner to see the play "ART," and I learned that Helen was a modern art lover which certainly helped since that was the theme of the play.

Helen and I began to spend more and more time together. I enjoyed her company tremendously. She was positive, cheerful and confident and we always had so much to talk about. Our work, our families, our backgrounds, which were so different.

It was still only just over a year since Marion had died yet I did not have even the slightest feeling of guilt. I talked to Marion as I had done ever since she died. She had always been wise and knowing and I felt that I would be pointed in the right direction or alternatively turned away from my present path. I could only be guided by how I felt, and I felt so good about Helen and our relationship, that I really felt that Marion was giving me smiles of encouragement. I also realized that this approach was rather convenient and somewhat self-serving.

It was time to introduce Helen to family and friends. Of course, when I invited my son and two daughters, my sister and brother-in-law and my best friend and his wife to an Easter brunch to meet Helen, everyone knew that something serious was happening. The occasion was a success—relaxed, fun and totally without strain. Everyone liked Helen, it was hard not to, and it was as though we had all been friends and family forever. Except for my son Adam. At the lunch he was fine but, like all of us, he was hurting from his mother's death and later when we met, he was more outspoken than his two sisters, one older and the other younger than he.

We met for coffee at his request, and he immediately took on the role of a father, something I found somewhat amusing.

"I just hope that you know what you are doing."

"All I know is that I am much happier now than I have been for a while."

He then went on about being cautious and not rushing into anything. I let him have his head since I felt that he really needed to play this authoritarian role.

"I feel your Mom's encouragement and that is helping me," I said.

"You don't know how Mom feels. It just helps your case to say that she approves."

"Possibly, I have thought of that, but I know her so well that I feel very comfortable with all of this, in fact more than comfortable."

"I just don't want you to make a mistake."

"Thanks, but I really don't think I will."

My daughters just wanted me to be happy and they could see that I was. They had been concerned about me, they liked Helen and saw our being together as being very positive.

Meanwhile, Helen was hardly biting her nails anxiously waiting for the next move. She was far too busy running her own business to worry about "will he, won't he" and besides, we were only at the beginning of a relationship with no question of any real commitment at this point. She seemed quite happy with the way things were going. Still, you could feel that the natives were restless.

Helen and I were doing all the New York things—movies, theatre, museums… I was beginning to enjoy them again, something I could not do, no matter how much I tried, after Marion's death.

I was due for another visit to my family in the U.K. and I asked Helen if she would like to join me. I thought long and hard before I did, knowing that I was crossing over a very important line. She had a son in London, and she gave me a very enthusiastic "Yes."

"Why don't we sail over on the QE2?" I said.

"What a lovely idea. If we are still speaking after seven days together in a cabin, perhaps we do have a future after all."

Upon arriving in Southampton, we made our way up to London to meet her son Stephen, his wife Stephanie and Helen's three granddaughters. They made me very welcome indeed and we spent a very pleasant weekend with them. We then left for Liverpool to meet my family and a different situation entirely.

My four brothers and their wives had known and loved Marion. They had known her before our marriage, and we had all spent so much time together before we left England. It was almost impossible for them to imagine me with anyone else. The fact that it was only 18 months since her death hardly helped the situation.

On the first night in Liverpool, a Saturday, we decided to meet at the Victoria Memorial Hall, the local working men's club that my brother Stanley managed. As was the custom, the women all sat together in a banquette with the men facing them. Poor Helen was in the middle. Although everyone was polite (not a good sign), Helen couldn't avoid the stares from various relatives who seemed to regard her as some alien being, and someone who did not belong. It made her very uncomfortable.

It had always felt like the prevailing belief in Liverpool working-class culture was that when you lose a spouse after many years of marriage, you are expected to go it alone. Even death does not allow you to part. It's very much frowned upon if the surviving spouse remarries, or so it seemed to me. This made my relationship with Helen so difficult for my relatives to understand. The fact that she was an American hardly helped the situation.

It was on this visit that the full extent of the differences between Helen and myself came home to me.

I was back in my working-class Liverpool home, where I had been born and bred. Seeing Helen, the sophisticated New Yorker and child of an affluent American family, in my environment brought out the stark contrast and helped me understand how difficult it was for my family. And it was also difficult for Helen, as I was to find out later in our hotel room.

"Derek, I'm sorry but I'm not sure I can continue like this."

"Helen, what do you mean by 'this'?"

"It's your family. I don't understand them. They look at me as though I'm from another planet."

"I get the feeling that you feel the same way about them."

"You're right, I do."

"I can assure you that things will get better."

Although the first meeting between Helen and my Liverpool family had been a little uneasy, all was not lost. There was another brother of mine who met Helen in New York sometime after. Here the outcome was quite different.

The phone rang in my apartment in the Olympic Tower on Fifth Avenue. It was my youngest brother, Robert.

"Hi Dedge, I've found a cheap flight and I'm coming over to New York for a few days with Peter (an old friend of Robert's.) OK if we stay with you?"

"No problem, Rob."

Our Robert, the youngest of the five brothers in my family, although having a history as something of a scallywag, was everyone's favorite. At the age of sixteen, he eloped with the girl he would stay married to for nearly 50 years. It was an amazing, loving marriage with his wife Ann giving him a free rein that was the envy of all his friends. He would take off for Europe to watch his favorite soccer club in a competition or flit over to New York for a short trip to see me. He always managed to scrape up the fare when needed. As far as Ann was concerned, he could do no wrong.

Despite his escapades he was not at all devious and in fact had a cheerful, sweet, almost innocent disposition and was always ready to offer a helping hand. My father often remarked how difficult it had been for him to punish Robert. Everyone liked him. He had an open approach to everyone and seemed to be quite at home with people of all types. Nothing seemed to faze him.

At this time in 1998, he was earning money doing small roofing jobs and living in a subsidized council house on an estate outside of Liverpool with his wife and four children.

I told Helen that my brother and a friend were coming to New York, and she immediately insisted that I bring them over to her apartment on 74th Street and York Avenue and she would entertain them.

On the first evening of their arrival, I took them over to see Helen. When Helen opened the door, she found a small, slight man with kind eyes and a big, warm smile looking back at her. That was our Robert. Next to him was a burly man with a blonde crew cut and a sallow, very pale complexion. In the interest of non-disclosure, I had not given Helen too much background on Robert.

Our Robert breezed in.

"Hello Hel!" (Liverpudlians have this penchant for shortening names.) "How are you"? No handshake or peck on the cheek. It was as though he had known her for years. Again, very Liverpool.

This was about 4 p.m. which to Robert and Peter was the bewitching hour for drinks, as was every hour. Helen had no such plan. She hadn't mentioned it to me, but she had arranged an elaborate afternoon tea-time, befitting the brother of the Englishman she wanted to impress. Out came the polished silver, along with her grandmother's Haviland china. All had been arranged in accordance with the Emily Post etiquette book that Helen had been studying all day, including whether the spoons were on the table or in the saucer. Her presentation would have put any Japanese tea ceremony to shame.

My brother and Peter handled it all so well, as though this was the way they had tea every afternoon. The fact that Robert and Peter usually drank their tea from a chipped mug only made my smile grow even larger.

Then Helen brought out her specialty of mushroom canapés and Peter and Robert tucked into them with a vengeance.

"These are delicious," said Peter, "but next time try them with a touch of garlic, I find that really helps."

That night Robert and Peter went out for a drink. Well, several actually. They were exploring the bars on Second Avenue and around 11 o'clock Robert decided to call it a day. Peter said he would stay a little while longer.

It was after midnight when Peter finally decided to come home. He made his way back to the Olympic Tower and tried to open the lobby door. It was locked. He walked over to the steps of Saint Patrick's Cathedral across the street from the building to figure out his next move. He soon fell asleep. He was awakened by something tapping the soles of his shoes. Peter looked up to see a burly member of New York's finest peering down at him with a baton in his hand. This man was a member of the NYPD that patrolled Saint Patrick's every night.

"Come on, young feller me lad, you can't sleep here. Better be getting home."

Without a word, Peter staggered to his feet and walked away and around the block. He decided to try the door again, but it was still locked. Feeling really, really tired, he goes back to the church steps and once again he falls asleep.

Again, the banging on his shoes.

"I won't tell you again. I've a mind to run you in. Where do you live?"

"Over there," says Pete blearily, pointing to the Olympic Tower.

"Don't you be getting cute with me. Now where do you live?"

When Peter insists on the Olympic Tower, the cop reaches down and frog marches him over to the lobby door. He then presses the night bell which Peter should have done originally.

The concierge came to the door.

"John," say the cop, "this feller says he lives here?"

"Oh, yes," says the concierge, "he's staying with Mr. Hughes, one of our tenants."

Peter staggered in the door and wobbled his way to the elevators and up to bed in my apartment.

That was my brother Robert's world. Despite his lack of funds he would continue to come over to New York as often as he could. Helen looked forward to his visits and, of course, so did I. It also helped Helen to understand my Liverpool roots and my family.

DO I HEAR A WEDDING?

In the fall of 1998, when Helen and I returned from England after our QE2 vacation, we had learned a great deal about each other. It was the first time since Marion had died that I had been happy.

I knew that many of my friends and family, despite the fact that they had been concerned about me since Marion's death, still felt that my involvement with Helen was a little premature. Some mentioned it. Some did not. Many felt, whether they expressed it or not, that my insistence that Marion approved was a little self-serving, as had my son. Others felt it a little weird.

Luckily, with a few exceptions everyone accepted Helen. The holdouts were people who thought that Marion could not or should not be replaced so soon. I moved on in my quest to woo Helen into marriage.

We saw a great deal of each other, traveled a lot, and our relationship grew and deepened.

Helen was still a little cautious about marriage. She had been single for 20 years after a very difficult divorce. She had her own executive recruiting company and a nice apartment on the Upper East side. She had four sons who were all doing very well in their respective professions, and she had a number of friends in New York and Connecticut where she had raised the family. Leaping into marriage with a well-married, heartbroken man was something to be considered very seriously.

Helen and Marion were so different and yet so similar in many ways. They were both blonde. Marion was rather shy and introspective. She had been burned in an accident as a child and although the scars could hardly be noticed, she was keenly aware of them, and this tended to feed her reticence. However, she had a fierce intelligence and was a top student at school.

Helen was American, privileged, upper middle-class to Marion's English lower working-class roots and yet it was so obvious to me that they would have been great friends. They have so much in common—a great sense of humor, an innate sense of goodness, and a love for all creatures great and small. They also both had that most important quality, that fail-safe against life's slings and arrows, which was an acute sense of the ridiculous. I had great fun picturing them whispering and giggling together in the corner. But then, oh my goodness, they are pointing at me!

I proposed formally to Helen at the Mayflower Hotel in Washington, Connecticut where we were spending the weekend in the Litchfield countryside she loved so much. With her sense of the outrageous she might well have said to my proposal, "You're joking, of course. Totally out of the question." After all, I had mentioned marriage when we were in England and her answer was "Yeah, yeah, yeah!" This time it was serious—she said "yes", and the nuptial die was cast.

Our friends and relatives were expecting our engagement, so although not universally embraced, especially by the traditionalists in Liverpool, it was no surprise.

When it came to the actual wedding plans, Helen and I had a very real difference of opinion.

"I think we should have a church wedding but with just a few people and a small reception—don't you agree?" said Helen.

I had different plans entirely.

"No, I don't see it that way. A church wedding, yes, but I want all of our families and friends with a large reception and celebration."

"Derek, this is a second marriage for two people in their 60's. Let's be a little more discreet."

"Helen, 'discreet' reads 'apologetic' or maybe 'furtive.' I want to shout our love from the rooftops and to hell with our age. Anyway no one told me that there was an age limit on romance."

"A lot of people will not be happy. What would Marion say?" Some might have thought that an unusual question, but not to Helen or me.

To answer, I reminded Helen how Marion when I first asked her to dance said, "You really think you're hot stuff, don't you?"

"Now what do you think?" I asked Helen.

"Marion is right. This is you. So, a 'Hollywood' wedding it will be."

The wedding would be at Saint Thomas Church on Fifth Avenue where I was a parishioner, followed by a reception at the St. Regis Hotel. When I arranged for my Liverpool family and friends to come to New York, I felt their disapproval dissipating and their enthusiasm growing. There's nothing like a good party to pique the interest of Liverpudlians, and they could see how happy and at ease I was. Besides, my brother had given Helen some great PR.

Helen and I plunged into all the details surrounding the wedding. It was very unlike me since I was used to delegating, but I relished it all.

The renowned Saint Thomas Choir of Men and Boys would sing with the church brass ensemble. Helen and I chose the hymns and also helped with the brass musical scores. I knew the minister who would officiate so that helped.

The church and the reception room at the St. Regis were to be decorated by a well-known New York florist, Preston Bailey. Nothing was spared. Oh, and yes, just to make certain I really went over the top, it was a black-tie affair.

Despite the many details and logistical planning, such as which guests would be invited, etc. there was very little tension between Helen and myself. We both knew what we wanted. A reverent but joyful wedding ceremony and a wonderful, no holds barred, "knees-up" party afterwards.

The church was decorated with beautiful spring flowers with a bowery of green at every pew.

As I stood with my best man and best friend Dave Saunders, looking out over the large congregation and

listening to the brass
ensemble as I waited for
Helen, I teared up more
than once. I could feel so
much love. There was such
a rightness of being about
the whole thing. One of
those very few, if any,
perfect moments in life.

"How do you feel?"
Dave asked. "Nervous?"

"Not a bit."

Derek at wedding reception, 1999

Helen came down the aisle between her two brothers
looking gorgeous and about 19 years old. The hits just
keep on coming.

Then it was over to the St. Regis to take care of our
200 guests. I was especially careful to make certain that
the bar could take care of the Liverpool contingent, who,
even when they have unlimited supplies, have been known
to exceed them.

Helen and I took a peek at the room laid out for
dinner. It was stunning. Every table with its own flower
arrangements and lighting. Preston Bailey had outdone
himself.

Normally at weddings the bride and groom make a
grand entrance and a big fuss is made. Not at our wedding.
When Helen and I walked in as the new Mr. and Mrs.
Hughes, the band was playing away, the crowd was on the
floor and the dancing had already started. Helen would
not allow me to grab the mike and shout "What are we,
chopped liver???" so we just joined in the dancing which
didn't stop all night.

We had decided that we would not have the usual wedding rituals such as tossing bouquets. If the women weren't married by now, well it's a little late, we thought.

The band seemed to be enjoying things as much as the guests and did not stop for breaks. The energy and fun seemed to sweep everyone along.

Derek and Helen at their wedding reception at St. Regis Hotel, NY, 1999

However, as so often happens with very happy, special times, the evening went by so quickly. Soon it was all over.

Could our marriage possibly live up to our incredible wedding?

Yes, absolutely!

As I write this, we have been happily married for 23 years.